THE
CLEAN
SLATE

By

Jim Clayton

BALBOA
PRESS

A DIVISION OF HAY HOUSE

Balboa Press books may be ordered through booksellers or by contacting:

Balboa Press
A Division of Hay House
1663 Liberty Drive
Bloomington, IN 47403
www.balboapress.com.au
1-(877) 407-4847

ISBN: 978-1-4525-1204-4 (sc)
ISBN: 978-1-4525-1205-1 (e)

Printed in the United States of America

Balboa Press rev. date: 01/08/2014

The wonderful lady who inspired it all,
my wife, Betty.

CONTENTS

DON'T MISS THE BUS

Chapter 1

I write this book of my life's experiences, assessment and thoughts, always searching for the truth and all for the sole reason to help young people around the world to cope with the most strangest and hostile environment the planet has ever experienced since humanity took over. A lot of young people especially in the western countries are living a life style as if there was going to be no tomorrow. With a recently estimation of 25 million unemployed in the world they may be excused for thinking the future is bleak. However, there is no need to throw in the towel just because someone predicts the end is nigh. When people talk about the end of the world, they are talking nonsense – the world cannot end – there is far too much resource under the lithosphere to replace the devastation that mankind has rendered to the planet's once pristine surface. That this unusual and strange civilisation must come to an end someday is inevitable with 8 billion of us coming up in the next 12 years. The world's resources are going to be taxed to the limit. So mankind, always the architect of its own misfortune, will as in the past, fight for those resources and the annulations of the human race will be complete and dear old mother earth will probably shake her weary body and say, "What a way to end it all!" as the cockroaches and other insects take over. So depending on the super power, someday there is going to be a clean slate and it will all start afresh. Right now there is still time, no need to panic. However to the binge drinkers and drug addicts, there is no need to read this book, because you have missed the bus you have just destroyed the world's most fantastic computer – the human brain! And no medical treatment can restore this delicate part of the human body. To those who are only on alcohol, and not yet addicted to drugs, there is still a chance of survival and catching that bus, if it's not too late and your liver is still intact. I enjoy a cool lager and a good wine now and again, but I cannot drink 8 cups of tea, so why should I be expected to drink 8 glasses of beer. Any doctor will tell you, alcohol should be taken in moderation or not at all. Alcohol is the most dangerous destroyer of all because it is legal and therefore is always available to everyone, despite some ridiculous age limit legislation which means nothing to 14 and 15 year olds. Drugs on the other hand are illegal and although huge quantities are confiscated in the war on drugs, massive quantities escape the net to destroy the brains of the vulnerable young and also the not so young. Mass murderers like Escobar of South America, who offered to pay off his countries debt if they would let him off, an offer the authorities must have turned down as when he was apprehended, he built his own prison from where he continued to run his drug business until he was finally shot by police. But not before he had wrecked the lives of so many people who had missed that bus. Making your way in the world today for young people is not easy. The two most essential requirements are good genes and good parenting. Without these you stand a good chance of missing that bus. However, you can still make it if you have the will power and the sense to resist the weak minded who try to make you join their self destructive throng. They have already missed that bus and are headed for oblivion. Not being a professional writer, I do not expect this book to even pay expenses, but if I can save the lives of just a few young people, then the loss will be well worth while. The youth of today are our future and there are millions out there who are going to make it. My hope is to see that that number increases. Around about 50 years ago, that famous American evangelist, Billy Graham, wrote a book named 'World Aflame". He related in the book an incident where a police officer climbed out on the edge of a skyscraper to stop a man from jumping to his death.

"Don't come any nearer." Said the man, 'Or I'll jump."

"Look", said the officer, "I'll make a deal with you. I will give you 5 minutes to tell me why life is not worth living. Then I'll give you 5 minutes of why it is worth living."

"Right, "said the would-be suicider.

So they both talked for the 10 minutes and then they both jumped.

I find that story hard to believe and it may just have been Billy's way of trying to convince his readers of what a crazy world we are all living in and that was over 50 years ago! Look at it now! It is 10 times worse. Throughout my life time I have often heard people comment that someone was born under a lucky star and wondered if there was any truth in it. It is a fact then there must be a lot of unfortunate people born under unlucky stars, like all the millions that are incarcerated in prisons around the globe. I myself have escaped drowning three times by sheer luck. I was never able to swim due to a lung infection when I was four years old. That left me short of breath and you certainly need good lungs for swimming.

The first brush with death was when I was 16 years old and was during the depression of the 1930's. The Acclimatisation Society had put a bounty on the big black shags that inhabited our lakes and rivers all because they ate the young fingerlings of the rainbow trout. So Joe Broughton, a young Maori I had befriended and I decided to go shag shooting to reap the one shilling and six pence bounty, to make some money as we were both out of work. Joe borrowed a 12 gauge shot gun off Tom Mc Donald, a local wine maker who he had helped with the vintage. Together we biked up to a huge lake named Ohiti that had many floating islands consisting of a native reed known as raupo. Joe and I found an old duck punt in the rushes and after emptying all the water out of it, we plugged up the holes with willow root and paddled out to one of the islands to hide in and so shoot a few shags. Just before we reached the island a flight of these shags came by and Joe in his excitement turned around in the boat too quickly to grab the gun, and overturned our flimsy craft. As the boat sank and we landed in the water, Joe called out, "Grab the gun. Don't lose the gun."

I grabbed the gun and called out, "I can't swim!" while Joe was looking under the water to salvage the boat. Then Joe called out, "the bottom is not too far,"

So I stood up right and touched the bottom. Being 6 foot tall, I was able to walk on tip toe with the gun held high and the water up to my chin, to the nearest island, praying that I would not step into a hole. I threw the gun onto the island, while Joe swam to it, stripped off and dived back into the water to retrieve the boat. We hauled the boat up and plugged the holes up with raupo roots and set sail for the shore with strict instruction from me for Joe to sit still. It so happened that there had been a prolonged drought that summer and the lake was well below its normal depth. So that was my lucky escape one, all due to a dry summer.

The second narrow escape was when as a fourth shareholder in a 28 foot yacht, with a 30 foot mast and a jib sail, the skipper who instigated the purchase and who was the only crew member who knew anything about sailing, had a girl friend who did not like the sea, so some weekends we couldn't go sailing. This upset the other three crew members who began to think it was a bad investment. I came up with a solution. I would ask my father who had sailed in England as a young man, if he would take our boat out and coach us. He agreed so the three of us mutinied and my father taught us the ropes even though the three of us were the real land lubbers who knew nothing about the sea and which we were soon to discover, was nearly our demise.

Dad showed me all the basics – how to turn about and tack, etc; then I took over as skipper. But we needed a crew of four, so we invited another friend to join us. One Saturday we were short handed so we invited a former skipper's brother to help out which he did, but brought with him several girls who had never been to sea before. So with one crew member short and all these girls on board, we set sail for the Pacific. Out in the bay quite a big swell came up and having never encountered such conditions before, I began to worry as to how I was going to turn about in such huge troughs. My ignorance and lack of experience really had me concerned. There happened to be a German freighter out in the Roadsted, loading wool by lighters towed out by tug boats as the port in those days could not take these big freighters. I thought, "I will get close to the freighter and turn about in case we have trouble, they could at least throw us a few life belts and perhaps save some of the girls."

As I began to turn about, no one released the backstay, which spills the wind as the boat turns and the boom swings out into the new position. Consequently, the boat heeled over and I thought it was all over. But a crewmember did release the stay and the boat came upright as it spilled all the wind. The merchant seamen leaning on their ships rail, watching us, must have thought we were all a bunch of no-hopers and of course, they were right. I did not like blaming the girls, but they were in the way of the skeleton crew. It was a good lesson to only sail with a full crew and fewer girls!

Another nautical disaster was averted some time later; however, this time we had a more experience, even though we all had still not earned the title of Able Seaman. One Saturday, afternoon, when all the boats were out sailing in our huge bay, we suddenly noticed we were the only boat left – the rest of the fleet had high tailed it to port. We soon were to see why. An immense cloud was fast approaching from the south, which meant a cold southerly storm; and by the time we reached the narrow opening to the channel and had a safe haven, it was too late. All we could do was to tack back and forth across the mouth of the harbour entrance hoping for a lull as the storm was blowing straight down the entrance. All the other yachties had come down to the pier to witness our ordeal, knowing we had a real task on our hands to enter such a narrow channel with no room to tack. A roar of cheers and clapping came from the pier and the crew all raised their hats in acknowledgement – but I was wondering if we had at last made it to Able Seaman, second or third class!

My final encounter with drowning was the night before duck shooting was to open in 1948. I decided to cut some long poles and drop them across the deep stream at its narrowest point, to catch any ducks that floated away. I was trying to push a long pole stake down in the stream to hold the poles and thought I had reached the bottom. I was pushing with all my might, when suddenly the ground gave way. It must have only been a ledge on the side that I was pushing the stake into and I went head first into, over three meters of fast running water. I had thigh boots on and as they were filled with air, I popped up like a cork and as I hit the surface, I saw the last rays of the setting sun on the distant mountains and thought this is my last view of mother earth! Suddenly, my head touched the pole I had placed across the stream. I grabbed it and edged my way to the bank. But I was in deep shock. When I got home and related my ordeal to my wife, she said," Well, that was one thing I thought you would never do – fall into that deep stream!"

I always figured that the events in one's life was either good management or bad management, I did not believe in luck, or in the case of Joe and I, plain ignorance, plus stupidity, as we naively expected a leaky old duck punt to carry us both in a bounty hunting venture. What if we had shot a boat load of birds? We just did not do our homework. In the case of the yachting close call, it was my lack of sailing experience and not being acquainted with the changing moods of the sea, plus the fact that our boat, The Illinois, that was her name, was not built for the open sea. A whole fleet of these boats were specially constructed for the 7000 acre inner harbour which was separated from the Pacific Ocean by a narrow, two kilometre long shingle bank. This huge inner lagoon was only about 2 metres deep and had numerous shell banks within containing all kinds of shellfish. Consequently, the boat had to have a steel central board that could be raised when negotiating these banks of shallow water. The boats had a nine foot beam and were flat bottomed and were called Patikis, which was the Maori name for flat fish or flounders.

With the advent of the Hawkes Bay earthquake in 1931, where the land was raised over two metres, this inner lagoon became dry. Consequently, the whole fleet of patikis were tied up until a few interested crews thought they would buy up these sadly idle boats and try them out in the main ocean. However, they were not built for such seas and so there were problems.

Although I strongly believe in fate and a destined road map, I have often pondered that this lucky star theory could be correct if my narrow escapes are anything to go by. If there are any such things as lucky stars to be born under, there must be a whole of a lot of unlucky stars when you take into account the immense number of accidents and other sources, where lives are lost at an early age. A close friend of mine, backed over a little toddler after making a delivery to a customer's household. The wee boy had wandered to the back of the van unobserved. My friend never got over that ordeal. Was this another case of being born under an unlucky star? Such an incident defies explanation.

At 92 years of age, I was up at my back country farm, repairing a washout at a concrete crossing in a stream that runs though the property when we ran out of materials. So to fill in the rest of the day, I decided to climb up a steep, bush clad hillside to cut up a tree that had been blown down in a storm and blocked the track that the cattle used to come down to drink at the dam, at the bottom of the hill. The track led above a deep ravine and I had walked that track for 40years and every time I had traversed it, I used to say to myself, "I would hate to slip and fall down there!" So at 92, that was exactly what I did. I had gone ahead with a chainsaw to cut up the tree and my helper was following some distance behind with a scrub saw. When I passed the top of the ravine, I grabbed at a branch of scrub to propel myself along, not noticing it was dead. The branch broke off and I dropped the saw and cart wheeled down into the ravine. My lucky star shone once again as I landed on a soak hole of water halfway down and that stopped my fall to the bottom where I certainly would have been killed! My helper heard my moans and groans and called. "I will get help!"

The locals all responded wonderfully with a blanket to keep me warm, as I was wet from the shallow soak hole. They assured me the rescue helicopter would soon arrive. The rescuers had quite a job in cutting a track out of the bush to get me to the copter, which then flew me to the hospital. The doctors were amazed at my quick recovery as I was walking again in a fortnight and was soon back at work, although still feeling quite sore in my shoulder and ribs. The doctors claimed it was because I was still working and so fit that I mended so quickly. When I was in hospital the nurses and other staff would ask me what the strange package was in my locker.

"That package is what keeps all my joints in good trim. It is ground linseeds, sunflower seeds and almonds that I sprinkle on my porridge every morning. It also helps me outdrive my accountant on the fairway, because I really need to because he cleans me up on the greens."

They all enquired where they could purchase the product.

When I left the hospital, they all came and thanked me for informing them of such a health giving substance. So lucky or unlucky stars, there must be some truth in it.

Now, take the Kennedy boys, Joe, Jack and Bobby. The three of them all lost their lives at such a young age, all in the name of public service. Joe with a plane load of explosives destined for enemy territory and which exploded too soon. Jack, by an assassin's bullet – a shocking end for a president, who with the help of Nikita Khrushchev saved the whole human race from nuclear annihilation, the military on both sides wanted to push the button. Castro flew into a rage; Krushchev was determined to have Cuba wiped off the map, just like Iran and North Korea are today. Then Bobby Kennedy; killed because he was out to clean up crime. Unlucky stars for all three that ended in a cruel blow for them and their families. Life can be so cruel, there seems to be far more sadness in the world than happiness, unless the good side is not reported so much. War, earthquakes, tsunamis, tornados, hurricanes, plane and train crashes, yet mankind pick up the pieces and carries on relentlessly.

Finally, I had no option but to believe in the lucky star theory because of the wonderful girl I married – she was not a lady in a million; she was a girl in a billion! Just after we were married, my father said to me," Jim, you have married a girl from an extinct species. When one of my son's marriage broke up, he said to me, "Dad, if I ever marry again, I am going to get you to pick the right one."

I replied, "Well son, I don't think I will be able to find you any one quite as good as I did." But what a wonderful tribute to his mother, who was a model of kindness and love, and who always put others in need before herself. I worked long hours each day for her so we could build the home she deserved and the best of cars I could afford and every time I bought a new car, she would say,

"There was nothing wrong with the old one!"

I would say, "Oh yes there was. This one has power steering, so you'll find it easier to drive."

Her mother's last words to her as she left her bedside, before she passed away were,

"Tell Jim not to work too hard."

I found it a strange how so many people tried to persuade me to ease up on the work, even my first ever bank manager said I was working too long hours, yet he died in his forties and I am still working at 96. Our body is like a battery - stop using it and it will slow down. So to all you youngsters out there, all your star needs, is a bit of polish to make it shine. There will soon be 8 Billion of us who will need a lot of food, clothing, housing, wheels etc – so take up the challenge. You will make it only if you contribute. Treat the world and your life like a band – nothing in nothing out! We only get out of life what we are prepared to give to it. If you are still not convinced in lucky stars, there is one more close shave I had with destiny.

I had just bought a farm off an old timer in the back country. He had an old dilapidated shed full of everything you could think of – he never threw anything out. One half of the shed was stacked with old newspapers and my eldest son and I were sorting through a lot of old tins to see if there was anything worth saving. I had picked up a large tin, but could not get the lid off. So I shook it to ascertain if there was anything in it. There was a clanging of metal, so I thought it must contain nuts and bolts. After a great struggle, I finally eased the lid off. What a shock I got! The tin was over half filled with detonators! We could have been blown to smithereens! I could not believe that someone could leave such dangerous contents unmarked. On the other hand, I heard of a soldier in the Maori Battalion who had survived the war, yet was killed while out deer stalking. He had leaned his loaded rifle up against a tree while he boiled the billy for lunch and his dog knocked the rifle over. It went off and shot him.

Fate plays some strange, freakish accidents in people's lives at times.

So to conclude, the main requirements need to catch the bus besides the afore mentioned genes and good parenting, you need will power, a sense of purpose, a goal to achieve, a good sense of humour, faith in yourself and most important of all, the right soul mate. Along with a philosophical outlook, that is being able to always face reality, because there is no substitute for truth. You cannot go wrong; you will be on that bus probably in the front seat. I cannot stress more emphatically how important faith is. Faith in yourself, faith in your soul mate, no matter what happens. I once employed five high school boys to clean and dig around my grape vines. I had a large valley planted in table grapes. I gave each one a sharp shovel and showed them what I wanted done. They worked well the first day, but unfortunately, it rained heavily for the rest of the week, so they were unable to complete the task. The next week, the soil being too muddy for them to continue, I journeyed into town to pay them for their days work. In 1949 the adult pay was around about two pounds a day, so I decided to give them a pound each for their days work, as it was their first ever attempt at work. One of the boys was not at home, so I gave the pound to his father, who grinned at me and said, "You don't mean to tell me, my son earnt a whole pound in a day! It is impossible, he cannot work."

"Well," I said," I soon showed him how and he was just as good as the rest, so I paid them all a pound each to give them some encouragement. It was just a pity it rained."

What I thought was so strange, was the father had no faith in his son; and faith is so important.

We once had a father plead with us to give his son a job to teach him how to toil. The father, who had no faith in his son said he would be happy to pay his wages if we took him on! I would not hear of it so I said, "If he is that bad, we have no place for him."

He turned out to be one of our best employees, honest, hard working and responsible. Here again, the father having such little faith, thinking his son could not perform. If a parent has no faith in their children, how can the children have faith in themselves?

I noticed one of the first things we had to teach young lads who worked for us, good manners. Some of them had apparently never heard the words "please" and "thank you."

When one of my daughters brought along the morning tea, she would ask if they would like a second cup of tea.

"Oh yes," they would reply. And she would say, 'But what do you say?" and they would look at her with wonderment, not knowing what she meant. Hard to believe that some parents play such an insignificant part in their children missing that bus!

You can never over estimate the immense power of faith. As an example, my youngest son, Mark, used to carry out the goal kicking for the rugby football team he played for. One game, when his team had scored a try and he had placed the ball in readiness to attempt a conversion, as he stepped back to take the kick, he was heard to mutter by the supporters on the sideline, "Gosh, what a long way!"

A big Maori man amongst the crowd called out," You can do it!" Mark gave it all the power he could muster and the ball sailed between the uprights (goal posts). He turned and grinned and waved his thanks to the man whose faith had given him the power to convert the try. Mark never forgot that man's faith. Maoris love their rugby and have turned out many, wonderful players. My wonderful wife taught me more about faith and loyalty than I ever thought possible to know and I'm sure it helped me surmount all the obstacles and setbacks I encountered through my life in reaching the goals I had set out to achieve.

I also have to thank my parents for the faith they had in me, through all my early years of childhood and the years that followed. I remember when I stated my first permanent job, at one pound per week; my mother said she would only charge me ten shillings per week board, if I would put away the remaining ten shillings in a Post Office savings account, which I readily agreed too. I am always so grateful to both parents for their part in seeing that I caught that bus.

Finally, if you do not have faith in God, at least have faith in yourself. Have a purpose, a goal. Do not set your sights too high, know your limitations. The peaks may be beyond you – leave them to the talented. Imagine the millions of little American boys who idolised Babe Ruth Lou Gehrig, Joe DiMaggio, for their baseball achievements. Even in my little country, George Nepia, Colin Meads and many other talented players in our world famous All Blacks, foot ball team who are idolised by young and old. So many talented players never quite make it, but come so close. But it is far more satisfying to have tried than to have cried! Still not convinced you have to catch that bus?

If you are young, you are in the most prime position to make your mark in the world, to reach a goal, be it ever so humble, it will be all worthwhile. Squander your health and you have thrown away that one great chance of achievement and joined the unfortunate throng of sad youngsters who have missed the bus by failing to realise that the excesses of youth are huge drafts to be paid at maturity; and the price is astronomically high. Here is a recent example where a young, bright girl did not even have to wait for maturity to pay for her excesses. A friend of mine had an extremely intelligent granddaughter who studied hard for her exams at university, passed all with honours, then decided to take a break for one year. Tragedy struck. She associated with the wrong people and is now a vegetable, confined to a wheelchair. She is one of many who had so much promise, but fell victim to the drug cartels that are destroying our youth throughout the world.

Decent, bright youngsters who have missed the bus. Even though she had been blessed with a chance of a lifetime, you can well imagine the agony of the whole family as they witnessed the destruction of a family member who initially had so much potential. Her downfall and sad mistake was taking that whole year off. A year, when you are young is a year lost, but in this case, it was a life time lost. Better to have been kept busy. If you're not busy then boredom sets in and the worst of human predators, the peddlers of drugs, pounce on hapless, unsuspecting young victims, who do not have a clue of the consequences.

During the good old bad days of the 1930's, that nobody wants to hear about, even though there were few jobs for adults and none at all for us youngsters, we were never idle. There is always casual seasonal work if you were prepared to do it. A few of us high school boys used to caddy at the local golf course. When there was no caddying, we played golf on our own course which we devised on some salt flats raised by the Hawkes Bay 1931 earthquake. The low salt weed was the rough and the bare long strips of dry mud flats were the fairways and greens. There were no green or membership fees and all were welcome. Some of the boys later turned out to be class players. Not me though as I was soon to get into the horticulture and did not take up golf again until I was in my 50's, so I never really reached the realms of being a good player. But I, along with my golfing friends and enormous amount of fun and I do owe a lot to golf because at about this time when I left high school and ventured into the second hand golf ball business. When there were no caddying jobs, the caddies used to go off to the rough areas of the golf course to hunt for golf balls. In those days there were large areas of rough, where hackers like I turned out to be, lost many a ball. In fact it was while I was hunting for balls, that I acquired my first golf club! My high school history master had sliced a ball into the rough and I went over to help him find it. As we both beat the top of the long grass with our clubs, searching for his ball, he noticed that my club was made of poplar stick, with a large knot at the end, a flat piece of lead nailed to the back to give some weight. I tell you, I could truly hit a long ball with that improvised golf club! But not as far as the driver I recently paid $700 for. My history Master, (Rupert De Worker was his name) noticed my crude poplar stick and said,

"Surely you can do better than that, Jim?"

"Afraid not, sir, "I replied.

"Come over to the club house when I'm finished and I'll see what I can do."

I could not get over to the club house quick enough, for fear I would miss him! He finally came out with a discarded hickory shaft drive iron of his wife's who was right handed. My Master had not noticed I was left handed as he was.

"Try this," he said.

"But, sir," I replied. "I am left handed."

Me and my first golf clubs. A present from my generous history master

Oh, that's all the better." And back he went in and returned with a three iron, a Niblick about an eight iron, a putter and even a bag! I could not thank him enough.

Anyway back to my second hand golf ball business. In those days, of the thirties, new golf balls like the best brands – Dunlop, Spalding, and Harleguin were two shillings to two shillings and sixpence each. There were twelve pence in a shilling. When I had found about 30 balls, I would cycle over to Hastings, a town 10 miles distant, to trade my wares to a cobber of mine, Percy Dixon who worked in his father's barber shop, lathering the faces of his father's customers who wanted a shave. Doc Dixon, as his father was known, had many of the town's well off business men, who played golf and as times were also tough for business in the slump, they were keen to pick up a bargain in the golf balls. Hence Percy had a good clientele. When I entered the shop with my current stock, I went behind a partitioned off area where Percy and I carried out our bargaining when he had a break from lathering his father's customers. While he was busy, I would arrange the golf balls in groups according to their grade or quality. A few new balls or near new, at one shilling, a few not quite so new, but in good heart – nine pence. Next grade at sixpence and the not so good, at four pence. These would be good enough for practice only. In between Percy's customers, not everyone could afford a shave, Percy would come and discuss the prices I had set and bargaining then would begin in earnest. It was like a game of chess, different balls would be transferred to other lots and we both used to laugh as I would transfer them back, as I knew their value. But Percy always knew just how much his clients would pay. We never, ever had an argument or harsh words and always finished up on a final transaction, we were both happy with. In between the bargaining sessions, they would often be interrupted with Percy having to attend to a customer and I remember clearly him enquiring to a client, Charlie Slater, of C.H. Slater Ltd, a huge fruit and produce wholesaler market where I was later on to supply with thousands of pounds, then dollars, of produce for many years before they finally sold out to Turners.

"Would you be interested in any golf balls, Mr Slater?" I heard Percy ask Mr Slater.

'Oh, Yes." Mr Slater would reply. "What have you to offer?"

"I have some fairly new Spalding's and Dunlop's, if you are interested."

So Percy would make a sale there and then, even before we had finished bargaining. But I didn't mind, it was quick turnover and good for business in such tough times. We were so lucky in those days with no drugs, booze, drinking age was 21 - no jobs but still plenty of positive things to do. It was so easy to catch that bus! Today with such artificial prosperity, cyber space, I Pods, EPods, Smart Phones – plastic money, it is all so unnatural. It is too easy and the youngsters get caught and miss the bus.

This chapter would not be complete without the wonderful story that my secretary has just revealed. She had just finished a sewing project when she realized she had made a mistake, so stayed up until midnight to correct her project. She listened to an amazing program on TV. about a group of intellectually disabled people; one had Autism, another two had Downs Syndrome and another had Foetal Alcoholism. They were encouraged, by a support worker to form a band and write their own music and lyrics; and then perform live to audiences. They travelled the North Island performing at different music festivals and other venues. They also released an album. Through faith and courage, willpower too, these wonderful people are reaching beyond their dreams. So listen up all you healthy youngsters out there. These disabled people had no ticket when they came into this world, yet they all caught that bus – just think about it. Hats off to those wonderful people of the support group, who made it all possible and hats off to those brave ones who against all odds, caught the bus!

BECOMING A GROWER

Chapter 2

In the early 1920's most fathers in the community finished their weeks work at noon on Saturday morning and after they had journeyed home, had their lunch, it was customary for most dad's to tend the vegetable garden to contribute a good supply of fresh vegetables for the family.

My father was an excellent gardener and we had a big section of ¼ acre with highly productive soil. When I was just five years old, I was following my father everywhere in the garden as he toiled, planting, hoeing and cultivating his crops and asking questions – "why do you do that?" or "why do you do this?" in childish curiosity as that is how children learn. I must have been getting in his road so much that he suddenly exclaimed, "Look, here is a packet of radish seed, I am going to give you a little piece of land you can grow these in and you can have your own little plot of vegetables, would you like that?"

"Yes, please." I answered. To have my own garden! I was so excited. My father dug the soil over for me and hoed it up finely, and then I went ahead and sowed the whole packet of radish seed. I could not wait to get up early next morning to see how my garden was and if anything had happened. Childlike curiosity got the better of me as I scratched the soil to find out if any of the seeds were doing anything. Lo and behold, the seeds had swollen in the night in the warm, damp soil. Convinced they were on their way, I replaced them carefully and patted the soil and my amused parents bade me to be patient as seeds needed time to germinate. Another day, without looking, was agony! I wanted to know what was going on under the soil, so on the third day I investigated again and I was amazed to find the skin had broken on some of the seeds and their size had increased dramatically. The fifth day was even more startling – a small shoot had emerged and my father advised that they would be better left undisturbed or they might not come up. Then after several days I perceived the ground cracking and then finally rows of little radish plants burst forth to my great relief and pleasure. I cultivated the soil in each row to keep the weeds down, then one day when the plants were quite big, I accidently pulled out one with a weed and lo and behold, it had a little red and white bulb on it! I was hooked! I ran and showed it to my mother, with such excitement, "Look what I've grown!" My mother smiled at my pleasure and complimented me on my achievement and from then on I kept weeding and thinning the crop until I had decent sized bulbs that were big enough to eat. That was eighty nine years ago and every spring; I still plant this same French Breakfast brand of radish seeds in my home garden. Of course, as I grew in those days of childhood, I branched out into carrots, parsnips, beetroot, cabbage, turnips and it all added to my dad's contribution to the family's food requirements.

Then in the 1930's when I was in Form 2 at the Taradale Primary School, each Form 2 boy was given a little plot of land in the school grounds to grow vegetables of their choice as an exercise to be judged at the end of the school year. The school had plenty of land in those days, even a large horse paddock as some children who lived in rural areas, came to school on horseback. Furthermore, the school also had a vegetable garden where we senior boys grew large crops of onions each year for sale to help school funds. However, the small plot idea was a new venture to test the ability of the individual. In this exercise, the Form 2 boy could choose a Form 1 boy as his assistant, so as to help the Form 1 lad in the art of vegetable growing. In those days each Friday, the boys were occupied gardening while the girls had sewing lessons. My choice of help was a Maori boy named Moana Tareha, whom I had befriended. Moana and I planted Swedes, carrots, turnips, parsnips and beetroot. We chose these root vegetables because we knew they would all mature in time for judging before the school broke up for the Summer holidays. Imagine Moana and my surprise when we were awarded first prize for our efforts. Little did I realize that one day I would acquire, by sheer hard work, saving and investing, over a hundred acres of alluvial flat land soil, 540 acres of fertile volcanic hill country where I could produce seed potatoes and also become President of the New Zealand Vegetable Producers Federation; and preside over my first conference being opened by the Governor General of our country!

However, to go back to those early days of my childhood, a great deal had to be learnt and achieved. My parents were not well off and there had been an economic downturn after the end of the First World War around 1922. My father told me that it was well known that British Majors discharged from the army and not being able to find work, were trying to sell matches on the streets of London for a penny a box, just to buy bread! However, I was just 9 years old before I was to make my first business venture. I had always been in the habit of rising early in the crisp autumn mornings to go out in the fields near our home to gather mushrooms for my family. Many times I would have surplus and would give them to friends and neighbours who would reward me with reciprocal gifts of fruit like apples and grapes. Then one morning I came home with half a kerosene tin of perfect button mushrooms as the delicacies were so profuse, I only picked the finest quality. When I showed them to my mother, she exclaimed, "Wouldn't the greengrocer in the main street of Napier, (our closest city) love to get his hands on these!"

"Oh, please, could I take them to the shops?" I asked.

She replied that it would cost nine pence a return trip.

"I've got nine pence in my money box, Oh, please can I take them?"

"All right," my mother replied, (she was quite an astute business woman and who had always taught me to save my money.) "But make sure you do not sell them for less than four pence per pound!"

So off I went with one of mother's clean tea towels covering my mushrooms, down to catch the bus to town. I sat behind the driver with my precious wares sitting on my knee. A man across the aisle spoke out, "Watchca got in the bucket, sonny?"

I was too nervous to answer, but the fellow passenger sitting next to him spoke up and said, "Tell him to mind his own business" This made me more nervous than ever, as all eyes seemed to be on my bucket of mushrooms, and I wondered if I had done the right thing in venturing out on my own. However, I let most of the passengers alight first as I did not want anyone to bump my precious wares and damage the quality. Walking up the main street, I soon came to the first greengrocers shop, so full of apprehension and hope; I nervously placed the bucket on the counter and began to remove the cloth. My head only reached the top of the counter and as an aging Chinese gentleman peered down at me, he said in broken English, 'What you got?"

"Fresh mushrooms," I replied as I removed the tea cloth.

"How much you want?" He sternly enquired.

"Four pence a pound," I replied.

"Three pence," he shot back.

"Four pence." I insisted.

"Three pence halfpenny." he offered.

"Four pence," I insisted.

"No," he replied, "Only three and halfpenny," he insisted.

"Thank you but no thanks," I replied as I placed the tea towel back over the mushrooms and made for the door. There were six more fruit and vegetable shops up the street, I knew I had the goods they wanted and I was determined to try the lot before selling them under four pence a pound! Halfway out of the shop the owner called out, "Come back here, I give you four pence – when you get some more?"

We became good friends and I kept him supplied as long as mushrooms were available.

Early mushroom days.

Later mushroom days, field mushrooms on our chevy loaded for an early morning trip to the market

I had learnt my first lesson in marketing. Only sell top quality to be a price maker instead of a price taker and I have followed that rule for over 80 years, as at 94 years of age I am still producing fruit and vegetables; and although many people try and talk me into retiring, I tell them how lucky I am to still be able to work and inform them that it is not the money, as I have far more than I need, it is for my health that I still keep going. Getting back again, to those childhood days, one New Year's day after we had had our new year's dinner, it was 1929, I was just 12 years old and my mates had all gone out visiting with their parents, I felt lost for something to do, and as I wandered out the front gate looking for company, I observed a Chinese market gardener who had rented 2 acres of land opposite our home, off the vicarage who owned it, picking by hand a crop of beans. After watching him for a while, I enquired, "Do you need a hand?"

"You pick a bean?" he queried.

"Yes, I said, "I can pick beans."

"I give you 6 pence a tin," he offered.

I readily accepted and as it was 2 o'clock by this time, I worked until 6 o'clock and had picked 6 tins of beans for which he gave me three shillings. When he paid me, he asked me if I would like a job working in his garden which I readily accepted. He offered me three shillings a day which was good pay for a twelve year old boy in the twenties. By Saturday, I had earned 18 shillings! I was the richest child in the village and I saved every penny! Other boys had paper runs which only paid two shillings a week. The Chinese market gardener I began to work for, knew my parents well because when they rented a property in Church Road for quite some time, they used to lease a few acres to the same man. Every Saturday night when he came home from his vegetable round in Napier, he used to pay me then give me a full sugar bag of vegetables, including a bunch of rhubarb which my mother used to convert into a delicious rhubarb pie, every Sunday morning. She would send me off down to see Jack Yee Ching (that was my boss's name) with this delicious pie as reciprocal thanks for all the vegetables he had given us. Jack used to be overwhelmed by my mother's kindness and he used to feast on the pie with great relish, while I talked to him. Then as a special treat he would play for me on his gramophone, a record of Chinese music, which I failed to appreciate having been brought up on Bing Crosby and Dick Powell.

"Do you really like that music," I queried.

"Oh yeah, "he answered, "Very good" and laughed at my astonishment. So just to please him each Sunday morning, I would stay and listen to his record while he consumed my mother's pie. My district was full of Chinese market gardeners, all living alone in their whares (small, one roomed shacks). I used to think what a lonely life they must have had. Jack had a wife and young son back in China and used to send all his earnings home so that they could survive and for the young son's education. What a tremendous sacrifice to make, never to see his wife or son ever again! Jack loved to show me photographs of his wife and son although as the little boy never grew up, he was the same age as my only brother. The boy finally became a teacher and then when the Japanese invaded China, became a soldier fighting the Japanese. Although I learnt a lot from Jack in the production of vegetables growing, I learnt far more from him about life. I discovered the great virtues of patience – there is no nation in the world as patient as the Chinese, hence their gigantic leap forward in industry. How to cope with adversity. I remember the years later when I was producing large quantities of vegetables and I was the president of the local growers association, we had a disastrous flood that wiped out the growers crops. I was appointed to a flood relief committee and I had a meeting with the local commissioner of crown lands who was directed by the central government to travel out of the worst hit areas to assess the damage. When he arrived on the scene, he observed all the Chinese growers dressed in oilskins and thigh boots toting shovels, trying to drain the excess water off the crops while the European growers were up at the local pub telling each other how much they were going to get from the Government. He must have put in a most unfavourable report because the only compensation that came forth was for the growers from a returned soldiers rehabilitation block where they had been settled on some low lying floodable land. There is no other nation on earth that can cope as well as the Chinese in adversity; floods, famine, earthquakes, typhoons, invasion that has been their lot over the centuries. Such disasters have taught them how to survive. I always observed when they lost a crop through hail, frost, flood or drought; they simply disked or ploughed it under and started again. I never ever lost touch with Jack and even at the end of the slump, when I finally acquired a permanent job in the building trade, I used to travel down to his garden after work to wash vegetables twice a week at one shilling and sixpence an evening (15cents) as I was still saving up to buy the few acres, I longed to grow my own crops. By this time, 1937, the Japanese invasion of China was taking its toll and as I scrubbed away at the turnips and carrots, I used to ask Jack how the war was going and he used to say, "Oh, all right."

And I used to answer, "It doesn't look too good by the pictures each night in the papers!"

He used to reply, Japan cannot win in China, there's too many of us, anyway, big war soon!"

"How big?" I asked.

"Japan come down to Australia and New Zealand, you see I know."

"What will they do with us? I asked.

"You have to work for them for nothing and they might not let you marry until you are 50 years old, so you cannot have children!"

He proved right except that America stopped them at Midway and the Coral Sea. Jack was quite upset when I informed him that my older brother, Sydney, had lost his life bombing the Japanese base in Rabual, New Britain (a captured Japanese stronghold) in 1944 as the American's were pushing the Japanese back in the Pacific. Sydney's remains were not found until 2001, as a USA War Graves Commission were searching the Pacific for lost flyers, they came across the crushed Avenger Bomber and seeing it was an American plane, assumed it was an American crew. They took all the remains to Hawaii for forensic Examination and found it was from N.Z. Air Force, so returned the remains to New Zealand for internment in the Military Cemetery in Bourail, New Caledonia. As I could no longer travel and had two grandsons in the N.Z Air Force, one was able to attend the ceremony on behalf of my family.

Flying Officer Sydney Clayton, died in combat in the Pacific War 1944

When Jack finally passed away, I could not help feeling sad for such a man that dedicated his whole life, working in a foreign land, to provide for his wife and son, he would never be able to see again – such sacrifice and dedication.

I will never forget one of the main lessons I learnt from Jack. The benefits and rewards for honest had worked. At the back of Jack's market garden was a huge swamp and one moonlight nights as I was returning from duck shooting in this swamp, I took a short cut through Jack's garden to reach my Harley, when I came across Jack cutting cauliflower by the full moon for his round next day. I put my gun down and held the sack open for him to make the packing easier and he was most grateful. Jack, my family and I had been friends for life.

It was around this time that I was to receive my first real break in my own vegetable production. An elderly widow, who lived across the field from my home, must have been impressed as how I was always working in the market garden, came to me and enquired if I would be interested in a small plot of land of my own. I enthusiastically informed her I would be most interested. She there upon offered me a small section of land at the rear of her property, about 1/8th of an acre which was covered in high blackberry bushes and huge boxthorn trees. She said I could have the land for free to grow vegetables as long as I wished if I was prepared to clear the area of all its noxious bushes. I jumped at this offer and thanked her kindly. So with an axe, a shovel and an adze, I went to work every week end. The boxthorn trees were the hardest to eradicated, as they had huge trunks that were really hard cutting and the foliage had the most devastating thorns you ever saw. However, I persevered weekend after weekend until I finally got the land cleared to burn. I did not realize that while blackberry and boxthorn were not deciduous they still shed an enormous amount of leaves each year which over time had added a great deal of leaf mould as natural compost to the soil. The next step was how to prepare the soil for planting, the plot was too small to hire the local teamster contractor with his big Clydesdales, and so the only alternative was to dig the whole block by hand with a shovel! As spring was approaching, I needed to get cracking or I would be too late for an early crop. So, weekends and at night after my daily work, when the moon was full I would toil away at my project. I remember one moonlight night when I was engaged I heard a familiar pudder, pudder of my cobber's Harley Davidson, coming up our street and pull up outside my home; and upon being told I was working over in my section, he trudged across the field and enquired,

"What the heck are you doing?"

John Stetson was his name, and we used to go deerstalking together. I explained to him my project and piece of land one day I hoped to buy. He then tried to coax me away, explaining there was great dance on at the Greenmeadows hall and named a few special girls he had a crush on that would be attending.

"Sorry," I said, "You go and enjoy yourself, I have a timetable to keep or I will miss the spring planting."

Reluctantly he sauntered off, leaving me turning over the sweet soil in the moonlight. I grew early Red Hubbard pumpkins and received top prices for they were of such good quality, grown in such virgin soil. I was in business, even though so small. Then a joiner friend, whom I used to travel to work with, asked me if I was interested in taking a quarter shares in a yacht. I hummed and hared for sometime as the cost was two pounds and ten shillings. The boat was going to cost ten pounds. It was a twenty-eight foot patiki, which is the Maori name for flat fish or flounder. A whole string of patikis were produced in the early twenty's for well off business men of Napier for sailing in the shallow inner harbour lagoon of about 7000 acres, close to the city. They had a flat bottom and a steel centre plate which could be hauled up where the water was shallow. They were very fast as they skimmed across the water and held quite a few people, including the crew of four. I talked my cobber next door into investing in the project and Doug Stewart; the instigator talked another cobber, Noel Whiting who worked with Doug, to also join. The hull of the boat had lain idle in a backwater ever since the 1931 earthquake had drained the 7000acre lagoon, but the sails and mast and spars had been safely stored away. Most of the fleet of boats had been laid up as they were specially built for the light seas of the inner harbour, as it deemed the open Pacific with its heavy seas were too rough for this type of craft. Although two pound ten shillings made a dent in my savings, it turned out to be the best investment I had ever made, as Noel had a neighbour cobber, Tim Fourneau, whom he invited out for a sail each weekend. As I was the only one with a car, I had to go over to Noel's and Tim's place each weekend to pick them up and that was when I spotted Tim's sister, Betty! It was love at first sight! But how was I going to meet her? I knew Tim would not want his sister on the yacht that was sure, so I plucked up enough courage to go to the next local dance in the district, hoping she would be there. Now, I could not dance to save myself, even though I was tall – six feet, I had no practice. I could not lead and I was also nervous! Not a very good combination! To my great delight, she was there and I plucked up enough courage to ask her for a dance. I cannot remember how many times I must have trod on her feet, but she told one of my daughters later in life, she did not care; she just wanted my arms around her! I asked her if I could see her home, which she readily agreed. I thanked her for the evening and asked her if she would like to go to the movies the following Saturday. That was it, we knew we were going to be together for life, no more dancing, even though she loved dancing, just movies and outings! We went mushrooming, blackberrying and motoring around the countryside. It was the end of the sailing season when I had met my sweet heart and we had brought the boat up from the water and placed the hull on the sand banks while we waited for the wool store where Tom Cottrell, my neighbour shareholder worked. The idea was when the wool store was finally cleared of all wool bales for the season we were going to shift the boat into the store and clean up the hull and paint it ready for the next season. Alas, while we were waiting for the woolshed to empty, a spring tide came up and quietly floated the hull off the sand banks and it drifted out to sea and was wrecked on the rocks below the cliffs, north of the port. Perhaps it was a blessing in disguise, I'll never know because at about that time I had found an eight acre block of land in a frost free area, where I had always wanted to go and grow early potatoes and early green peas, which realised exceptionally high prices in the market because of their quality and earliness. The year was 1939, the price of the land was four hundred and fifty pounds (a pound was worth 20 shillings) and this amount was an enormous amount of money at that time, as the depression was only just over and this block had lain idle and unsold for over 15 years. No one had 450 pounds to buy it and no lawyer had the funds available to lend me, so I bargained with the owner for one hundred pound deposit and an interest and principle quarterly payment thereafter. Of course, I did not have the 100 pounds saved up; I did not want to sell my car as I needed it for work and to travel to the land I would be buying. Luckily by this time Jack Yee Ching had given up the two acres he leased from the vicarage; as we were loyal parishioners, the church was willing to lease it to me. I knew I could save and earn the deposit if I planted crops in the two acres. I planted early dwarf tomatoes, pumpkin, beans and watermelons and I had just started to pick the beans when a hailstorm with hail the size I had never seen before, wiped out the entire crop! I was devastated. My father had sold me two large apricot trees which were laden with large fruit, just ready for harvesting when the hail struck! That crop too was ruined. The hail storm was only a hundred yards wide and it cut a narrow swath through my land and a Chinese market garden in the next road and then petered out. It was as if I had been singled out for my first test of adversity! My philosophical outlook saw me through as I was determined nothing was going to stop me from buying that piece of land! But I was never going to have that one hundred pounds deposit in time. I was forced to bargain with the vendor again to reduce the deposit to fifty pounds. He was most reluctant, but finally agreed if my father would guarantee my transaction, which he did. When I took my sweetheart up to the land, the very day of the purchase after work and she perceived the view of the whole bay and city, she was over the moon and as we walked around the flat area at the top of the section, we were like a pair of mallard ducks, choosing a nesting site, as a large area had been previously excavated for a building. We then both began dismantling an interior fence line so I could engage a contractor to plough the whole block in readiness for planting. As the land had been unoccupied for the last fifteen years and had never been grazed, the pasture had overgrown, and unknown to me, been planted in an unusual type of grass named Poa Potensis, a species of couch grass that could stand any drought. This grass made ploughing extremely difficult to prepare the area for planting and later cultivating. In those days, seed merchants were most willing to give growers credit to get their business. I had previously dealt with both as they were excellent to deal with. Little did I realize the disaster which lay ahead for me as the potatoes came through the ground so too did this terrible grass, that I had never encountered before and the more I cultivated it, the faster it grew! I had bought an aged draught horse off one of my yachting mate's father. Collar, bridle, chains, single tree, haynes and the horse all for seven pounds ten shillings, a bargain I thought, yet still a big outlay for me just starting off. The problem was I could not use a scarifyer to cultivate the crop as this type of couch grass developed into a mat like wire netting, so I had to employ some mates of mine at sixteen shillings per day, to help me hand hoe the crop. Despite our efforts, the tough grass beat us as the more we hoed it, the faster this couch like grass grew and outgrew the potatoes. Here's me with one bill of twenty pounds and another bill of twenty five pounds owing for the seed and no crop to pay for them! This also meant that I could not leave my job as I had intended to operate full time, on the land. My only hope was the early pea crop, which had fared much better than the potatoes. However, disaster was to come here also. Owing so much money for the seed potatoes and not being able to leave my job, I was not there when the peas were ready to harvest and the birds devoured the crop while I was at work trying to earn money to pay for the seed potatoes!

The old ways in the 1930's. Clydesdales discing
the land in preparation for cropping.

However, this was only the start of my problems, as in the course of all these events my sweetheart wanted to become engaged to me on her next birthday, which was in May; and even though she was twenty one, she wanted to do it all properly and requesting me to ask her father for her hand in marriage. My fiancée was the most wonderful daughter any parents could have wished for, she taught at Sunday school, did the housework, did all the sewing for the family, milked the cows, etc, etc. Imagine her bewilderment when her father refused on the grounds of "not while there was a war on!" My girl was devastated – we only wanted to become engaged, as I was too deep in debt to be able to build a home and also I was already in the territorials as I had joined the army when I was seventeen years of age. It so happened we had already ordered the engagement ring and had paid a deposit of two pounds as it had to be altered to fit my sweetheart's finger. The ring was to cost ten pounds.

What will we do?" she asked me, "They cannot stop me getting married!"

I thought for a while, as I had not expected such a big step while at the same time I had launched into growing crops and things weren't looking too good!

DIAMONDS VERSUS FOUR BY TWO

Chapter 3

"Well," I said," As things are so tough we could forgo the two pounds deposit and spend the rest of the eight pound deposit on four by two timber and build a small dwelling that I could one day turn into a home.

"Oh, you do not have to do that," she replied, "I'll come up and live in a tent, if you like."

"Oh, no," I said, "You cannot do that."

"Why not," she asked, "Plenty of pioneers started in a tent!"

"Because," I explained, "You cannot catch rain water off a tent to drink." There was no water on the property so she understood.

Now, not to be deterred, I started building the concrete foundations for a sixteen by twenty four feet small dwelling for us to start life together. I really had my work cut out trying to tend my crops and erect a building at the same time. Winter was approaching so I could not start at 4am and put in a long day – there seemed nothing but hurdles as it decided to rain every weekend. How well I remember, trying to put a coat of plaster in the back wall to hold a barge board to take the spouting to run every drop of water into our recently purchased water tank. Just as I finished a heavy shower came down and washed the lot off. I remembered the story of Robert Bruce of Scotland and the spider as he sat in his hideout on one of his many defeats; I carried on and put on another coat of plaster. When the weather cleared, those stories we learnt at school were a great help. Thank heavens I remembered, the "Try Again" story of Robert Bruce. We had decided to get married in September as the green peas and potatoes, if there were to be any, would be ready. Not knowing the pitfalls that lay ahead, we were both full of hope, despite my wife's family's opposition. Yet everybody that knew us was overjoyed at the thought of our union -all my friends and my parents and my boss and all my fiancées friends (as she was such a popular and highly respected girl). As the time approached for our wedding day, her father's best friend could not believe that he would not attend the wedding and give her away, so he paid her father a visit to try and talk him around, but he would not budge! My boss could not understand it at all either, because he had great respect for me and helped me no end, I could not have had a better boss, and he even gave us his palatial beach home for a honeymoon.

So we had to elope, there was no other choice, we could not afford a wedding breakfast, yet the church was packed with friends and relations all wishing us well, but there were no festivities. Yet we were so happy to be together to start out in life.

When we arrived home from our honeymoon, we only had six shillings and seven pence between us and the floor of the dwelling not paid for – but we had such faith and hope in each other we were really the richest couple in the whole wide world! The first weekend we were home, fourteen friends called to see us in our little ranch and as we only had a small table and only two chairs, everyone was seated on bushel fruit boxes. Every time another car would pull up, my wife would say,

"Two more boxes please Jim."

And out under the trees I would go and fetch two more cases for them to sit on. They were all so pleased to see us and admired our little humble start against so many odds. Even the bosses son, Selwyn Boyles used to bike out thirteen miles at the weekends to help me build our little home. He used to visit and stay with us often later on, he used to love riding one of the draught horses; he was only sixteen years of age and like his father, a real nice guy.

Our first little home

As the time drew near to harvest, it became apparent that the potato crop was a complete failure owing to the noxious grass ruining this yield. With the birds devouring the pea crop, the yield was well below expectations, even though the returns for the peas we sold, was high. With the potato seed still to be paid for and no crop, and this land quarterly instalment still to be met, our finances were really stretched. I bought an old rugby car off my father for ten pounds that I was going to convert into a small truck to take the produce to market. However, not having much produce and needing the money, I asked my father if he could sell the truck for me as I no longer needed it, which he did, but the buyer did not pay him. My father gave me his address, I called on him for payment, but he had vanished so now I had neither truck nor money.

Just another hiccup in our monetary difficulties, yet my wonderful sweetheart never once complained, we just overcame all the hurdles together and carried on. We could not afford electric power when we first moved in, as that would have meant expensive power poles, so we used candles and cooked on an open fire. For baths we went down to my people's place and to do the weekly washing also, until I built an outside laundry. My first priority was however to get rid of the terrible grass that had ruined my potato crops. This I could only accomplish in the dryness of the summer. So all through the hot months I disked and scarified and harrowed until my arms ached, to kill this terrible grass. Getting rid of it all was the turning point in our venture as the following season we grew a smaller acreage and received a much better return. However, another hurdle appeared as the Japanese bombed Pearl Harbour and came close to Australia. I was called up into the army just as my crops were ready to harvest. The army put our unit on the rifle range right away telling us we had better be able to shoot, but it was too soon for the city lads as only three of the whole company hit the targets! So they transferred us to an artillery unit, hoping we would do better, with bigger weapons. At the same time I entered the military camp in Waiouru in the high Central Plateau of the North Island near Mt Ruaphehu, six hundred re-enforcements of the Maori Battalion also started training. They were from remote areas in the East Cape region and some could hardly speak English, but they were keen to fight and were a really great bunch of men. They arrived with a complete instrumental band from bassoons to trumpets, saxophones clarinets and trombones. They took over the Y.M.C.A and gave all the lads great entertainment which was greatly appreciated. I ran into a young Maori boy whom I had befriended and who had worked at a dairy farm as a welfare trainee. I only knew his name as 'Bill". Bill had apparently lassoed a policeman while riding through the streets of Ruatoria on his horse. The place is a real hick town miles away from anywhere and was known to be quite unruly similar to Tombstone or Abilene in the USA in those good old cowboy days. Bill was not really a bad guy, I found him always friendly and pleasant, but the police did not take kindly to his action, so sentenced him to work on a dairy farm as a "ward of the state". The new input of Maori lads did not take kindly to the harsh discipline of the permanent staff English Army sergeants and the punishments they administered to these lads. So one night a group of Maori recruits lay in wait for one of the tougher sergeants to teach him a lesson. The sergeant put up one heck of a fight, but was overpowered by numbers and given a real beating. During the melee, he must have dislodged two buttons off one of the Maoris' great coats as the next morning, before parade, it came over the loudspeaker that all Maori reinforcements were ordered to parade in their great coats. Believe it or not, 600 great coats had two buttons missing!

With 10,000 men in training in a confined area, it was not long before a dysentery epidemic broke out which was devastating. Then an influenza epidemic hit the whole camp in which I was involved. However, the overzealous doctors in their endeavours to bring us back to fitness, made the almost fatal mistake of removing my sceptic tonsils while I was getting over the flu, the result ended my training as a soldier and I was discharged to produce vegetables as a war effort, but it was almost a year before I was even well enough to perform the tasks as I had contracted yellow jaundice after the operation.

With another season's crop lost due to my army call-up and later being discharged in the middle of winter, it was back to square one. Meantime, my horse had died, I was weak from the operation, the only money available was my army pay cheque, which was eighteen pounds– but I still owed hundreds. My solicitor advised me I could get a soldiers financial assistance, but I refused, being determined to make it on my own, as I had little respect for welfare, I did not even accept the child allowance for our first born, claiming I was capable of providing for my family without the Government help. However, my accountant insisted I accept it as I had been already taxed for it. When finally, my health returned and I was able to work the land again, I had no horse or no money and was back to square one. However, I contacted an Agricultural contractor who had a large team of Clydesdale draught horses to plough my land, but his brother had been called up in the army. He said he would work my land if I could give him a hand to build dams on some adjacent farms and also help him cut chaff and work on the stationery threshing mill. As all this was important, essential work, I readily agreed, of course I also needed the money if I was to fulfil my obligations to produce vegetables. I envied Jack Johnson (that was the contractor's name) and his great big Clydesdale horses and longed for the day when I could afford one. When working on the Mount St Mary's Mission farm, building several dams, we built a large corral with feed bins made of sacking, where it was my job to fill each bin with chaff, while Jack followed me with a bucket of oats and added a small tin of this extra grain to the chaff to make sure his horses were adequately fed. One evening after a hard days scooping earth for the dam we were building, all of a sudden there were horses screaming, biting and bucking. I high tailed it over the feed bins to escape the flying hooves. All Jack did was to yell at the horses, "Cut it out, you silly so and so's!" He never moved an inch and all the horses quietened down.

"What on earth was that all about?" I queried.

Jack explained that in every team of horses there is always a boss and a horse called "Knobby" was the boss. What Knobby was doing, was checking each bin where the other horses were eating to see if their bin had more oats in them than his, when suddenly all the other horses objected and so the outburst.

Motorization in the 1940's – Clydesdale horses
with sledge, implements and family.

It was not easy producing crops during the war as petrol was rationed; and you had to have a permit to purchase all fertilizer and shotgun cartridges for pest destruction. As we progressed I was able to purchase three big Clydesdale horses and do all my ploughing and cultivating. By this time, my father -in-law had come around and given us two little Berkshire pigs and Betty's mother had given us half a dozen chickens, the only trouble was, my wife had to run down to the fowl house every time a hen cackled after laying an egg or my hunting Irish Water Spaniel would beat her to it as he knew what these hen's were cackling about. Then after one year, we managed to save up enough money to pay the mortgage off the land and my solicitor said to me, "There you are, now free!"

I asked him how much money we would need to buy Amy's house and the seven acres, next door, which had been on the market since before the war for 2000 pounds.

"None at all," said my lawyer. "Go home and tell them you can buy it."

A mid-winter crop of lettuce grown in a field of composted, threshed, rotary hoed oats and hay

By this time we had a young family and I needed the extra land for our horses and crops; also there was a need for a larger home, ideal for our growing family.

My wife and I with our first born, son Barry.

I could not get home quick enough to tell my wife the good news and she could not believe it. It seemed too good to be true, so over I went to see the neighbours to inquire whether the place was still on the market. Unfortunately, they said, "No." as the son explained to me, the shift would be too much for his aging mother. When I went back and broke the sad news to my wife, we were both shattered as we had had to wait so long. When the property was for sale, we did not have the money; but now we did have the money to purchase the property, it was off the market. We did not know what to do, whether to wait or build as our family was growing larger. I had built a small sun porch onto our little dwelling for the children, so we could perhaps wait a little longer. Then a new option came up. A block of 12 acres came up for sale right next door to our eight acres, with a better building site for 600 pounds. I said to my wife, it will have to be your decision as the purchase would once again delay building a new home. Her immediate answer, without any hesitation, was, "get the land!"

Her wisdom knew no bounds, as after a few more years of increased production, I scooped an excellent site with my Clydesdales and started building a large home of heart timbers with such a magnificent view. I had to have a break in construction as I had a large, early green pea crop to harvest and I had 16 pea pickers.

Early spring green feast peas, just ready for staking.

It was the days before frozen peas were available and I had just purchased my first new truck, a 1946, one ton Ford V8. It was the first new truck to come to my province after the war. I had found a new market for my peas in the city of Auckland where they could not produce peas as early as September, whereas I could pick our first peas in August. The only trouble Auckland was a difficult destination to send to as the produce had to be transhipped by train and sometimes the connection was missed, so I decided to transport them myself. Quite a formable journey over two mountain ranges, steep winding, shingle roads and a distance of 300 miles. It used to take me 10 hours there and 9 ½ hours return. I used to leave at 8pm on a Sunday night and arrive in Auckland at 6am Monday, unload, have breakfast and drive straight home – starting to nod off 60 miles from home, I'd pull up and have 20 minute sleep, then drive on. But man oh man! Did I sleep when I got home! However, I had to do it as I was building such a big home and needed the money. Not even borrowing any to start building, as I was doing so well with my peas on the Auckland market – they being the only peas on the market floor. On the way to Auckland with our first load of fresh peas, we stopped at Hamilton about 4 am for a bite to eat in an all night cafe and parked on the opposite side of the road. When Colin Wood, the young lad who worked for me and who had accompanied me on the journey, returned to our truck, a policeman and a night watchman who had hidden in a shop door way by our parked truck, came out of the shadows and enquired about what we had on board. When we told them, it was a load of peas; they tried to persuade us to leave them in Hamilton as the price would be good. But I refused as I knew that all the main Hamilton buyers would be in Auckland on a Monday. When we reached the Auckland markets and I backed into the loading bay to unload and saw the big sign Produce Markets, where I had been sending small consignments by rail and doing so well, I saw alongside their premises another big sign, "Turners and Growers Ltd"

I thought perhaps I should have been sending to both but it was too late now. I was well established with Produce Markets and I did not want to appear disloyal or dissatisfied. I had to admire the way the wholesale market arranged the consignment. They placed two bushel cases of peas in front of every row of vegetables to hold all the cities buyers who were bidding on all the other produce and were waiting to bid on each of the two cases of peas. I could not get over how they sold the peas; taking farthing bids which was extremely astute and why they realised such high prices. Being the only peas on the market and all on the one floor, made a great difference to Turners, as they had no peas to sell, I had the market to myself, right through September and early October. This was too much for the Turners so down they came to see me, Sir Harvey Turner himself, his brother Del and his Hastings Manager who knew my operation, and Ross Walker, his right hand man. I had a block of big winter lettuce growing in front of the house I was building. As we walked passed the house towards the green pea block that they were anxious to see, Ross Walker nudged his boss and said,

"Harvey, look here, he is building this house himself."

"Huh! Anyone can build a house. Look here!" as he pointed to the lettuce crop of summer lettuce.

Sir Harvey was such an astute business man; he was only interested in the crops. To me, I thought my house was my greatest achievement. I thought anyone could grow lettuces, but no one could build a home like I was building. One builder friend of mine said to me when I was showing him though the house,

"Why have you used so much timber – I could have built 3 houses with what you have used."

My answer was two words, "Strength and earthquakes!"

Sir Harvey begged me for some peas, but I said, "I am sorry, Sir, but I would l feel so disloyal to Produce Markets, if I gave you some."

"We admire you for that, "he replied," but we have got to have those peas!"

Scooping the site for the second home

Our second and last house that Jim built

When I refused to alter my consignments, Sir Harvey decided to take action and he sent an agent down to our district to encourage all the local pea growers to consign to his market and engaged a local carrier to transport the peas to his market.

He engaged a well known transport company, McDonalds Transport Ltd. Ron McDonald, the head of the company rang me saying, "Jim, you will not need to go to Auckland this weekend as we have a truck going through and we can take your crop."

"How much are you taking," I enquired.

"Six tons," he answered.

"Oh well, I will be sending very little, if any." I well knew, six tons of our districts peas to Auckland, was six tons not going to the capital city, Wellington's market!"

I always believed in keeping a finger on the pulse of the market, if I was to stay in business and this latest piece of information confirmed my decision to send my peas to Wellington. As it so happened, on my latest trip to Auckland, as I backed up to Produce Marketing landing, a Chinese market gardener who originally cropped in my district and whom I knew quite well, had shifted to Pukekohe, (a large cropping area close to Auckland) and he had backed his truck in alongside mine, came over and asked me what I had on board.

"Peas," I answered.

"All peas?" he shot back. "Why don't you try other side?" Which I knew meant Wellington.

"No good," I replied.

"You try?" He said.

"No, Willie, Auckland the best. Auckland two shillings per pound. Wellington only one pound."

"Well," he said," I got my first 20 cases today, and next week, big pick."

It was valuable information to me. Auckland peas coming in a rush and Sir Harvey's six tons from my district, was a recipe for a crashed market, so I sent my peas to Wellington, at less than half a penny per pound freight, by rail; and received one shilling three pence per pound. In Auckland, owing to the large local supply and my districts six ton load, they reached only 9 pence per pound, minus 3 pence per pound for freight as it was such a long journey to Auckland. It was simple arithmetic of supply outstripping demand; and you did not have to be that bright to read it.

I could not see the reason for procuring the entire crop of peas from my district for the Auckland market, just as the local Auckland pea crop was coming on stream. The entire output from such a large pea growing districts was just too much to absorb, hence the market crashed. The pea growers from both districts must have wondered what on earth was going on. I suppose I got the blame for not giving any peas to Turners, but they really picked the wrong time to flood the market. The whole unfortunate scenario reinforced my theory, that you do not make money by just producing horticultural produce. It boils down to how you sell your produce. Marketing is the name of the game and the key to it all, is quality and continuity of supply of this high quality.

The glut of potatoes was caused mainly by the entry of many unprofessional potato growers entering in the industry at the time when horticulture took off and became the trendy occupation to be in. As an example, my eldest son, Barry called on his local dairy one lunchtime and the lady behind the counter said," Just the man I wanted to see!" and rushed into the kitchen to bring out a saucepan of mashed potatoes. She thrusted them under his nose and said," Barry, tell me what is wrong with these potatoes?" Barry knew his potato varieties backwards, took one look at them and said," Arran banner! Poorly grown."

He actually knew the grower who had supplied the dairy. It was the easiest query he had ever been confronted with. The grower was new to the industry and had quite possibly irrigated too close to maturity, which was detrimental to the cooking and eating quality of any variety. But a real disaster with such a poor variety of potato as Arran Banner. The grower concerned became a close friend and informed me years later that he had so many complaints, that year that they had to reimburse a distant wholesaler of their entire consignment to preserve their name. Their action paid off as they changed their variety and production methods. I had to admire them for being so honest to admit their mistake and make good the loss their customers suffered. I know of potato growers who have lost their chipping contracts simply because they have irrigated too close to maturity causing their product being unable to be chipped. It simply stand to reason, if you irrigate any crop, especially potatoes anywhere near maturity, you are undoing the immense work of the sun on the leaves that produce the starch and sugars so vital to flavour and nutrition, which is all the result of photosynthesis of the sun's rays on the leaves of any plants foliage. I have produced early potatoes on my home block for 73 years without any irrigation whatsoever and I have nothing but satisfied customers and a healthy bank balance to prove I am on the right track! Another example was many years ago the manager of our local Growers Co-op, Lou Lane, a close friend of mine and an astute wholesaler and judge of potatoes, rang me and enquired as to the variety of potatoes were we at present harvesting. I thought it rather an unusual request, however, informed him they were Katahdins, a popular American variety with shallow eyes and super flavour. He expressed his disappointment as he wanted them for his Taupo branch and he informed me he could no longer sell Katahdins in Taupo.

"Well, "I said, "it's all we have at the moment and they are selling well with repeat orders."

""Ok," he said," I will take a load, but I will not be able to call them Katahdins."

"Call them what you like," I replied. "I'm sure you will get repeat orders." I do not know to this day what he called them- perhaps he used their American name, Chippewa. Puzzled at his request, I decided to investigate the situation. It so happened, that this variety has an unusual habit of while producing many good sized tubers, they also produce many small ones. The growers of course thought they would do something about all these little ones, so irrigated their crops to improve their size. They did a great job with the little ones, but destroyed the eating quality of the big ones, hence the customer rejection. Consequently, one of the finest flavoured variety ever produced, quietly faded away. We produced the variety right up until you could no longer produce the seed. Only one grower was left producing Katahdins seed and he even ceased soon after the year 2000. What puzzles me is it is so easy to produce excellent flavoured potatoes if you stick to the old rules. There was never this trouble with the varieties that are constantly added too as many of these new varieties had excellent qualities, some were only suitable for special soil types and conditions, where as with the old varieties you could grow then anywhere. After a lifetime of producing potatoes and encountering so many different varieties and strains of this ancient vegetable, I have come to the conclusion that there is no such thing as a poor variety of potato. There are certainly some a lot better those others. All types of potatoes can be excellent to eat if grown correctly. It is the growers who make the difference over irrigating too near maturity. No vegetable not even water melons can stand excessive moisture when the crop is maturing. Potatoes love a cool climate, we produce our best eating potatoes in the middle of the winter, but with plenty of sunny days to mature the crop. The best main crop potatoes with the best flavour are produced in the north island of our country are grown in the Ohakune district, a volcanic area close to New Zealand's most active volcano, Mount Ruaphehu.

*Moulding potatoes in 1940 with Clydesdales and
an American Planet Junior Culitivator*

*Moulding potatoes in 1950's with a modern
tractor with a hydraulic cultivator*

The high altitude with summer sunshine and ample natural rainfall, the
quality of their crop is assured. The wholesaler, retailers and consumers
I had spoken too in Auckland, our largest city, where most of Ohakune

crop is sold, all testified to the excellence, edible characteristics of this districts potatoes. When potatoes are correctly produced, as they reach maturity, the tuber emits a strong potato aroma and the first to pick it up on our property are the pheasants. Pheasants love potatoes, in a frenzy they scratch the top of the mounds with their claws until they unearth the top tubers and devour them to their hearts content. They were so bad one year, that a potato producing family complained to the local Acclimatization Society and the society told them to take a petition around for all the growers to sign and then they would see what they could do. However, some of the growers like me were game hunters and did not mind sharing the crop with these birds as we were quite partial to roast pheasant. I think the outcome was the society came up and fed the pheasants maize hoping they would lay off the potatoes for a while. We also did not want the pheasants exterminated as they are our best earthquake recorders/warners. The moment mother nature begins thrusting any given quantity of magna up through the earth's intricate system of conduits towards the earth's surface, the pheasant s in every part of the property give out a loud distress calls and warn us of the slightest explosion. Even though the pheasants still devour our potato crop, I no longer shoot them as I like to see the male birds and their pretty plumage, strutting around with their hens and chicks in the spring. But they are still among my best customers for my potato crop.

To prove again how important the sun and low rainfall is at maturity is to all crops in our country experienced the worst drought in 70 years in 2013 and the fruit had the best flavour ever! In previous years, when we have been harvesting apricots and there had been significant rain in the night, the next morning the flavour was gone.

My eldest son would call out to me, "have you tried the apricots today?"

Actually, I never tasted any of the varieties that we now grew for the markets as they were large and very pretty, but poor in flavour. I always chose the old varieties like Moorpark, Royal Steven's, Favourite Newcastle and Hemskirts that the birds tore to shreds as they devoured these delicious varieties. The birds never, ever touched the new ones the supermarkets liked because they were big and pretty. I called back to Barry, "No, I suppose the rain has destroyed the little flavour they did have."

"Yes, he replied, "You would not know what you were eating."

Yet by 10 am with the sun on their leaves, their slight flavour had returned. My barber is a great fan of field mushrooms and one day he asked me why field mushrooms had more flavour that cultivated ones.

"Simply because cultivated ones are produced in the dark with no sunshine, where as field mushrooms, that may only receive two or three hours of sunshine, make such a difference. Never under estimate the immense power of the sun in the vital part it plays in all crops to enhance flavour and nutrition.

Thinning early apricots

I once took a case of tree ripened Newcastle apricots into a close friend of my son who was a retailer just to give him a treat and to remind him of the flavour of the old variety. He was busy serving a customer when I entered the shop, so I placed the box on the bench. A lady entered the shop and spotted my apricots and began bagging some – she had recognised the old variety. I sadly informed her they were not for sale, as I had brought them in for the shop keeper's family. She apologised and put the apricots back. I was so sorry; if I had had more in the car I would have given her some. It was such a shame all these old varieties that gave the apricot its popular stance in the industry will be gone forever from the market but not in my orchard, as I still produce them for family and friends.

Erosion is the penalty for cultivating warm, sunny slopes in wintertime

There are a lot of kind, hard working, honest people in horticulture who think they can escape the hard business decisions and fluctuations of the market by joining a growers Co-operative. However, they fail to realise that their co-ops has to deal with and overcome the same difficulties the market place continuously provides as all wholesalers have to cope with or they would not be able to survive. A Growers Co-operation in a huge production area was not doing so well so decided to engage a new manager who was not experienced in the industry. He approached a friend of mine, Lou Lane, an experienced, astute manager of our Local Co-op, in which I was once a Director. On explaining his new position, he asked Lou if he could give him any advice.

"Certainly," said Lou, "When soliciting supplies off growers for special orders, where-ever you see Turner, the largest and most successful advice – Do not pull the lion's tail! The new manager heeded Lou's advice and did extremely well. Except he failed to heed that last piece of advice and he did pull the lion's tail, resulting in the big firm closing him down without a blink of their eyelid. Years later, when no harm could be done, I related the incident to Jack Turner, one day when we were having a chat. He laughed and said, 'We wondered why we were losing quite a lot of business at that time!"

To prove how vital the combination of the weather plus that unpredictable and puzzling element of human behaviour, is to the outcome of the market place. I relate the following – I was invited to an all male evening to wish a young local farmer all the best for his forth coming marriage. Although I knew most of the guests, I chose to sit at a table with two of my neighbours who had just launched out into horticulture, John Gunnel and Jock Stevenson. John was really a pastoral farmer and Jock was a top class journalist and reporter of our Daily newspaper. Neither had the background for such a precarious, hazardous industry as horticulture. I knew both were not doing so well and had encountered the same problems I had endured when I first ventured in the hillside cropping in the district. John had bought a larger property than mine with a home and also leased quite a large area, while Jock was on a smaller property. I put the question to them, "Do you ever consider share cropping?" John and Jock gave each other the strangest look that puzzled me. Then John spoke up and said. "I will talk to you later."

When John came up to see me one day he explained how he and Jock, who was his brother in law, had been in shares that season hence the strange looks! And it had been a disaster, so they had both decided never ever, to go into shares again! I then explained to John who had so much land, that I had markets begging me for produce, I could not supply. Alan Simm, general manager of Townsend and Paul, in the capital city, was pressing me hard one day for increased supplies and he said, almost accusingly, that I sent a lot of produce to Turners and Growers. I replied, "Alan, I cannot afford not to send to Turners."

"That is the best recommendation I have ever heard from a grower about a produce firm."

It was for this reason I explained to John that I had the markets I could not supply and he had the land. If we combined it would benefit us both. So he provided the land and his labour, while I supplied the finance, machinery and extra labour and trucks. John had a herd of dairy cows, but it was really not good dairying country – it dried out in summer, producing little grass for the herd, but great heat for maturing early pumpkins and tomatoes. Our first crop was early tomatoes so we worked up a hillside, then the next day I arrived with my team with the plants and fertilizer and took one look at the slopes and instructed which way the rows would run to avoid sideslip during cultivation; we spread the fertilizer, rotary hoed it under and had all the plants in by smoko (morning tea time). As we quenched our thirst John exclaimed, "I can see how you have got ahead so quickly – you look at the slope and made a decision and the project was underway, where as Jock and I would have argued for an hour as to the best way to run the rows. Then he said," Oh well, it's too late to start now, let's go home for a cup of tea!"

After planting a decent block of tomatoes, we continued to plant 10 acres of Golden Hubbard pumpkins and Red Warren Squash. One morning when John arrived at work, it was getting near harvest time for the Golden Hubbard's; John said that he had some real bad news. John Marshall, a neighbour with just a small backyard garden had sent away his first seasons early pumpkins and only received six

JIM CLAYTON

shillings a sack. John was full of concern for himself. He was worried about all my outlay – how was I going to get it all back with such low returns!

"Nothing to worry about," I assured him. "John Marshall has tried to beat the gun. He has sent immature, early pumpkin to an over saturated market full of Winter Keeping pumpkins."

It so happened that the previous Autumn had been extremely dry, making the winter keeping pumpkins better as a long keeping proposition, with not so many going bad during the winter, therefore the market was over supplied and too many growers held on for a better price that was not forthcoming and were now panicking to unload. It was the old rule of mathematics again- supply outstripping demand!

"What are you going to do?" enquired John.

"Ride out the storm." I replied. "It will not take long, even though ours are almost ready. We are going to have to leave them to mature and harden, then pack them into large sacks and send them to the best market in the capital that is capable of reversing such a market upset."

"Who would that be?" asked John.

"Market Gardener Co-op," I answered. "Just you wait and see. I have been in this situation before. It is nothing new to me!"

John still looked worried so I further assured him, "Look, John. Our Hubbard will be so red, hard and mature; and so sweet and full of true pumpkin flavour, they will be sell like hot cakes!"

"For your sake I hope you are right," he replied.

Then when the Greys were finished we harvested three truck loads of really mature, top quality Hubbard's but bagged only one truck load and sent them to the Co-op, holding the rest to await results. 10.00am next morning, as we took a break from packing tomatoes, the phone rang, "Good news," I said, "It will be the pumpkin price. They have rung early – a good sign".

I looked at John, whose expression looked as if he was awaiting a death sentence. I excitedly picked up the phone. "Could I get another load down right away?"

They fetched five pounds – that was 100 shillings per bag. I put my hand over the phone and called out to John, "A fiver a bag!" Of course he did not believe me – he reckoned I was joking!

From then on, it was truckload after truckload. We bagged at night and early morning when the crop was too heavy with dew to harvest. John's wife's brother came down from Wairoa to help, also his uncle and a cousin. They were all so pleased John had struck the Jackpot! But not so the neighbour! Word got around and some had stopped waving to John when he met them on the road.

"What strange behaviour, you would think they would be pleased!"

As I have already said human behaviour defies analysis.

As the cheques rolled in, John surprised me. He began to spend it all. First he painted the roof of his house, then the whole house, then all the sheds, then all the gates! However, I thought it a bit too much when he had battens near the gate painted too! I began to warn him it may not be as good as this next year. It was then that he told me, he had the place on the market, as he wanted to move on. John had taken advantage of the wind fall to spruce up his place to make it more saleable. The price for the pumpkins did not drop until quite late in the season. One day, when we were still packing tomatoes at a good price, the phone rang for an order for pumpkins at two and a half pence per pound John could not work out why we should stop packing tomatoes at a high price to pack pumpkins at such a low price.

"Several reasons," I replied. "First, this firm obtained such high prices early on, secondly. It is an order for the Wellington Hospital, thirdly, it is still a payable price and we should be grateful to receive the order and most important of all, we have a duty to keep the market supplied, especially in my case, where I am in the business for the long haul. John Finally sold out and went back to his real love sheep farming, as he was best at that. I finished up buying some of the land and leasing the rest. As we predicted that next season, every man and his dog produced pumpkins. Orchardists, with bare land, farmers with a tractor or two, even a fisherman in our district with several trawlers, had to join the bandwagon. Of course with such unprofessional production and packing and with so many new comers, trying to beat the gun, the market collapsed causing them to drop out the following season, while the stayers, like myself who could weather the storm throughout my early years of such experiences, I came to realize that there was no one more efficient than growers to ruin a market! At grower's meetings, the producers always blamed the wholesalers for crashing the market, but I used to point out to them that is was the Growers who gave the wholesalers too much product in the first place. When I travelled around the world and perceived the massive amounts of produce available in all the big cities, I realized why they mostly sold by private treaty, (that is a set price as they had far more chance of holding a payable price, not a high price), than if sold by auction and it was because there was such an enormous continuous supply. A general manager of a large market in California took me down to a huge warehouse cool store stacked to the roof with cantaloupes. As he opened the door to show me the contents and perceived some over ripe melons, he exclaimed," I told him to quit this line! "They were unsalable. I wondered what would happen to such a large line that had been top quality when first available, but was in over supply, I found my travels around the world that growers everywhere all had the same problem, how to get an adequate return when there's a huge surplus that tumbles the market. Horticulture is one of the easiest industries to go broke in, on account of the risks faced in production and unpredictable market. So with John and Josh back, doing what they were so good at and what they loved like the Montana cowboy who refused six million dollars for his ranch because he loved his horse and his dogs far more and plus 85 years tilling the soil, it is not really the monetary return that is most important. While the revenue is vital to survive, it is really the goal of achieving what you have set to conquer that is the greatest reward. Money is only the route of all evil if you do not know how to handle it. With JPMorgan, Carnige and Rockefeller, it was not the money it was the power that the money gave them that intrigued them. Looking back over the years the best part was when my wife and I started life together and had to surmount the hurdles the setbacks and the challenges in the industry. Our humble little home was only a glorified shed, but could have been a thatched hut; it would have still been a palace to my sweetheart, simply because I had built it after we were married.

My father said to me, "Jim, you have married a girl from an extinct species!"

One of my son's whose marriage had fallen apart said to me, "Dad, next time I get married, I'm going to get you to pick my wife." A wonderful tribute to his mother.

Some of the gladioli bulbs grown to give to friends

I replied, "I will have a hard task to do that if you want someone as good as your mother!" I suppose that was why I worked day and night to be worthy of her and to eventually provide the best for her and the family.

But it was those first years when the children were so young and we were all together that were the best years. I always pointed out to my children that their mother was the most important member of the whole family, that without her, we would all be lost. I always insisted the first ripe apricot, nectarine or plum, no matter who found it, it had to be given to mother. However, it generally I who picked the first plums but there would only be two or three really ripe ones and when I presented them to her, as the first of the season, she always held the first one out you me and said, "Here, you grew them, you have the first bite."

"No, no," I would rely. "I had the first bite out of a worm eaten one before I threw it away." Now there's a strange act of nature when a caterpillar enters a green fruit, the plum even though green as grass, immediately begins to colour and ripen around the entry point. It is because the progress of the fruit to reach maturity has been interferred with, just like the branch of a fruit tree that is going to die. The fruit ripens first. It is the old law of survival. Our children always followed my example of giving their mother flowers, even though they had no flower garden like mine. However, there used to be a wild flower growing along our roadsides with a large yellow poppy like bloom that wilted the moment you picked it and that the three girls used to constantly bring to their mother. She could not thank them enough for the blooms and always had the entire kitchen window sill filled with all the children's contributions. It was a case of leading and following by example. Children always mirror the parents and that is why good parenting is leading by example. If the parents are into alcohol, don't expect the children to be tee totallers. If the parents are on drugs, the children will be also. I thank God every day for the parents I had and the values they taught me. So I could pass them onto grand children and great grand children, to be so proud of.

*Children from my old primary school, with their
teacher having a lesson in horticulture*

*My youngest daughter, Christine, with her pet
deer who followed her everywhere.*

So what do you really need to succeed in the horticulture industry? Not much more than in any other calling. Honesty, hard work and dedication to your customers, plus a love of the soil which you should leave in a better heart than when you found it. Keep replacing the fibre soil structure so it retains natural moisture and thus save massive over irrigation. Always remembers the old adage – 'The hoe is better than the hose'. In the marketing of produce you have the producer, the wholesaler, retailer and most important of all, the consumer. However, when packing each container, whether they be bags, cartons or bins, the grower must always be thinking, "how would I like to retail and sell what I am packing to the toughest inspector in the world – the consumer, who knows just what he wants and what he is prepared to pay for it." And at the same time, the retailer must still make a living doing it. That is why you cannot afford to pack anything the retailer has to discard, because if you do have, you have hurt yourself more than anyone and your productive operation will surely fail. I was in shares with a grower in a pumpkin crop and he handed me an immature pumpkin. (I never put my label on any produce I did not grade or pack myself) I asked him, "Surely you would not eat that?"

And he replied, "I would not eat any of them."

"You are not much of an ad for the produce," I replied.

So if you satisfy the consumer you are sure to please the retailer and then the all important wholesaler will worship the ground you walk on, simply because he can recommend and guarantee your product. I mention all this important consideration of the final procedure in marketing first to save any would be keen horticulturalist, all the hard work and investment in producing their first crops because if they are not prepared to meet the total industry's requirements by neglecting any of these essentials is to jeopardise all your efforts and investments. To succeed in horticulture you have to be a confirmed optimist. You must be able to cope with any type if set back, like hail, frost, wind, erosion, If your farm slopes, fluctuating markets, inept Governments, both right and left administrations that can throw immense hurdles in the path of your production, thought up by their bureaucratic advisors, to make life more difficult. The resource management Act is one such measure that comes to mind. If you can cope with all these, the rewards are immense and the satisfaction immeasurable.

My family, bar one with our wonderful Ford Mercury car.

BUYING A FARM

Chapter 4

The market returns for the 1969, late spring and early summer had been the worst ever recorded. Top quality, 20 kilogram bags of new potatoes were sold in the local market for 20cs per bags. During the '50s and 60's, horticulture experienced a boom with such returns every man and his dog wanted part of the action. Even the professionals could not resist buying up tracts of land without really knowing what to plant and with not an inkling of knowing where they were going to sell the produce grown there.

I had numerous approaches and enquiries from many would-be horticulturists. I tried to explain to them all that you do make money out of producing horticultural crops you can only survive the occupation in the way you sell the produce – marketing is the name of the game.

Doctors, Lawyers, accountants, even jewellers, invested in land for the purpose. Land agents had a ball even selling a lot of highly marginal land to unsuspecting buyers who knew so little about what they were getting into.

It so happened at the time that the Pip Fruit Industry was the most popular to enter. This sector was under Government regulation. During the Second World War, when shipping space was short, the Pip fruit industry faced disaster as the growers depended on export, so with the lost European markets and shipping space, the Government came to the rescue and guaranteed the price to all Pip fruit producers to keep the industry from collapsing. At the end of hostilities, the producers were so content with the arrangement they wanted to keep the system going even though the war had ended. From then on a body known as the Apple and Pear Board had complete control of the entire crop, both for export and domestic consumption. So with the strict quality standards, plus the single desk selling system, the Board brought prosperity to the whole pip fruit industry.

On a New Zealand Fruit Growers World Tour that my wife and I joined, and which was made up mainly of Apple producers, we found that our countries Apple and Pear Board's, one desk selling system, was the envy of pip fruit growers worldwide. When we visited Wenatchee, the apples growers in British Columbia, their producers had just been on strike. In the hall where we met the growers, there were placards they had marched down their main street with. One read,"5cents per pound or on the ground!" another "I have the apples, but I have no money!" and so on. In the Okanagan Valley, it was similar – a struggle to maintain an adequate return. In the apple capital of the world, Yakima, in the State of Washington, we could not have met a nicer bunch of growers, their hospitality was boundless. Wherever we went, the United Kingdom, France, Germany, Italy, South Africa, and Australia – they all knew about the success of the Apple and Pear Board and its selling system.

We found that the producers worldwide, all had the same problems, how to reduce the overdraught, how to pay off the mortgage – how to replace the living room carpet! However, it appeared, that to achieve those aims, the New Zealand marketing system was the best way. Perhaps because New Zealand is a very small fish in an extra large ocean, the demanded pooling of the entire crop to enable the community of supply, plus a quality product, it gave the Board such marketing clout. However, with such excellent returns for the pip fruit, especially apples, the bonanza began to attract the non professionals. A typical example of a new comer, not knowing what to plant, was a close neighbour of mine who was an expert panel beater and had invested in 6 acres near my property and built a palatial home. He decided he would grow a crop of onions. The virgin soil, having never been cropped before, naturally produced top quality onions enabling my neighbour to make a reasonable job of grading and packaging them. He sent them off to the Wellington wholesale market where all newcomers thought you had to consign your produce. Upon receiving the sales advice of just 2 pence per pound, he rang me in a panic to see if it was possible to get his onions back. Sadly, I had to inform him they were irretrievable and that he should have rung me first so I could have put him onto a better market. In those days the Wellington markets were well known that when produce was short, the sky was the limit, but a dumping ground in times of glut. I told my friend to make money out of onions, you need to grow 50 acres or more and know just where you are going to sell them. He gave up growing and stuck to panel beating and leased the land to me where I produced a more suitable crop for the area.

Another neighbour, and extremely qualified optician, who had invested in a 30 acre block of land, decided to go into Apricots and Citrus. Without any knowledge of either commodity, he chose two varieties of apricots that were extremely subject to splitting if the weather was at all wet when the fruit was maturing. When this happened the wife rang me in tears, saying,

'Oh dear, the fruit will all be split and unmarketable. Walter (her husband) has gone back to bed!"

"Not a bad idea", I replied. I could not go 'back to bed' – I had no spectacle business to fall back on – I had to salvage what I could of this risky crop.

Although I did not want the headache of another block of apricots to look after, Walter finished up leasing the orchard to me. However, I took over the property for an extremely special reason. On the southern side of the orchard there was a large lagoon with tall reeds, commonly known as raupo in New Zealand; and where large flocks of wild fowl made their home. I had four keen duck shooting sons and a close friend who was an expert clay bird shooter who could join us in such an excellent shooting site. Kiwis, as we New Zealanders are often called, are renowned for getting there 'priorities right' and my boys and I were no exception.

I worked it out, the citrus block would at least pay the rent; if it was fair weather when the apricots were ready, well and good; if not we had even better duck shooting, we could just not miss. It was an ill wind that blows nobody any good.

Just in case anybody reading this epistle may be wondering, what on earth has all this got to do with buying a farm – well, it has everything!

It so happened that quite a few of these well off, would be horticulturalists, who bought up quite sizeable blocks of crop able land, went in for potatoes. The returns for the potatoes, especially the early crops, had been most rewarding for most seasons. Often some of these producers would approach me to buy their potatoes crop in the field, as they did not have the necessary machinery to harvest the crop and also would not know just where to sell it. When I turned them down they would exclaim, "But you know better than us where to market the crop".

I had to contradict them, "No", I would tell them, "I have no idea where to sell your crop, I only know where to sell my own crop."

I do not know what the edible characteristics of your potatoes will be, they may be good or they may not. With our crop, we used a high potash mix of two tonnes to two tonnes of phosphate and only one tonne of nitrogen, plus 500 weight of trace elements in the right proportions of magnesium, manganese, cobalt, copper, boron, sulphate molybdenum – all of which not only produce a healthy plant, but tubers of the best eating quality. As previously stated, the late spring harvest in 1969 and the early summer crops of 1970 were a disaster, these non- professionals flooded an already oversupplied market where the top grade 20kg bags of new potatoes, sold for 20cents per bag to be fed as pig food as there was no other outlet. Consequently, the next season, not only the fly by nighters as we used to call these non –professional growers, who were always chopping and changing, gave up. The professional growers hit hard by the low returns also reduced their acreage. The signs were so obvious and this is why the marketing had such a human input. The weather certainly plays an important part, but the human reaction to the market is the most important.

I once asked a large prominent grower friend of mine in the South Island who produced massive quantities of main crop potatoes for the North Island winter consumption, "Why do the majority of your producers in the South Island, choose to sit on their large stocks as the moment the price of potatoes start to rise they quietly feed the market and so make a good cash flow?"

His reply was, "So you and I can make a milking!" This reply of course was the result of the procedure, not the reason. I could only surmise that the main reason was because the South Island main crop potato growers were also farming stock, grain, grass and clover seed. Their potato crop was just a side line that they could afford to play the market with.

A full time vegetable and potato grower has a duty to supply the market if he wants to acquire the loyalty of his wholesaler, which is so vital to the success of his operation. Only by constant communication with your wholesaler can you feel the pulse of the market and so be able to supply the correct quantity and receive an economic return. I once was invited to present a paper on a large scale market gardening operation in New Zealand on behalf of my Growers Federation, at a Massey University Agricultural Science Conference. I continually emphasised the importance that a large scale vegetable producer could not afford to refuse a payable price; and his constant contact with his wholesalers were the key to this end. Also the only way to acquire the loyalty of his wholesaler was to be able to supply top quality and continuity.

I remember an instance years ago when Turners and Growers were struggling to build an auction market in Hastings. It was a formable task and only Turners were brave enough to tackle the venture. The market showed a loss for the first few years, then one autumn, Ross Walker, their astute manager, bought Eddie Lays huge onion crop.

Eddie was a most successful onion producer, but never ever held on for the last dollar or pound as it was in these days. Eddie sold the whole crop for a good return to Turners. Whether Ross Walker knew something or took a big gamble, we will never know, but the firm made 9,000 pounds – an enormous amount at that time out of those onions. It was the first time the market had shown a profit. At last the firm was really established. Eddie had got his payable price and never regretted the deal because he was an excellent business man. As Rothschild once exclaimed when commenting on buying and selling shares, "many investors never learn the art of selling too soon. Waiting for that top dollar can be so devastating and disastrous!"

With the end of the 1969-1970 potato marketing being such a disaster, the "fly by nighters', gave up potato producing altogether. These unprofessional growers had their fingers burnt so badly they gave it all away.

The mathematical effect it was going to have on the supply for the next season prompted my company to increase acreage rather than diminish it. All the aforementioned experiences, history and repercussions from the events are documented to prove how fickle and difficult not only the market, but the whole industry can be. I could have easily been miles off course, if too many had done the same, however, the gamble paid off and I was able to purchase a sheep and cattle farm from the windfall we received for the following year's record prices. A disastrous potato season caused the following one to be lucrative.

The farm was by no means an expensive, well developed, high producing farm. That would have been far beyond the reach of a humble market gardener! The farm of 540 acres was a half broken in, low producing, almost derelict property with almost non- existent internal fencing, no cattle yards, a broken down wool shed and a house that would one day have to be bulldozed. Here is how it happened.

One evening, a land agent I knew well rang me to see if I was interested in a block of land in the Patoka district. "How much an acre?" I enquired.

"50 pounds per acre", the agent replied. "Sign him up!" I answered. "I'll buy it without seeing it." "Oh, you cannot do that", the agent said, "you have to meet the owner and he has to approve of you!" "Who on earth is the owner?" I asked.

When he told me who the owner was, I said to forget about it. I had heard about this old hermit up country and the many times he had buyers for his farm only to withdraw from the sale at the last minute. "No, no," cried the agent, "this time he is genuine as he has a bad leg and has to give up farming". I was still reluctant to be drawn into a wild goose chase with an impossible vendor. The agent, determined not to give up, queried me saying, "Surely, there would be no harm in coming up to look at the property?"

So being finally convinced it was worth a try, the agent, my eldest son Barry and I journeyed up to the property which was situated in an extremely popular and sort after district. Not only with a 50" annual rainfall, but was within the massive ash shower of the gigantic Taupo eruption; and I well knew what fine quality, main crop potatoes, volcanic soil could produce.

It was a cold morning and my son and I wore heavy winter jackets, known as Swandris. Trudging on foot, over the property, we had to take our heavy clothing off and my son folded his swandri under his arm. The flat paddock and gentle terrain really impressed us as did the rich volcanic loam. We ignored the state of the internal fences and the 200 acres of tall kanuka forest that would have to be crushed and burnt – to us it was only a challenge. All my son and I could visualise was the long rows of main crop potatoes thriving in that loamy, well drained, volcanic soil. – And countless mobs of wild ducks zeroing in on the small lakes, ponds and dams we would immediately be building.

Priorities! Priorities – always as true kiwis getting our priorities right! On reaching the home paddock, we passed a row of high pine trees and observed a low branch where the old farmer's turkey had roosted. I picked up a large, prettily marked feather and handed it to my son and said," Here, take this home to Michelle," his little daughter."

As we walked over the rise to the old farmer's house, he came over to meet us and without a word of greeting to the agent, pointed an accusing finger at Barry and exclaimed," I see, I see, he's got a turkey feather in his hand, what's he got in the swandri? Turkey eggs?"

I thought, "Good heavens, what on earth have we got here? I am going to have to handle this guy with all the expertise I can muster"!

After introductions were finally made, the old guy queried me,

"Well, what do you think of it?"

I had already chosen my exact words, the moment he accused my son of having his turkey eggs.

"It's a cracker," I informed him. "A wonderful property."

"You really like it?" he said.

"Yes, it's just what we want,"

It pleased him no end, so I knew that we were accepted. We had yet to see his old house and the woolshed. I could see in the distance the wool shed, with a broken back and later to find on inspection, holes in the shearing board and a dilapidated shearing plant. The house had opossums resting in the attic above the rooms where they had made nests out of the pine needles from the nearby forest, blown in through the rotting weather boards. There were bees nests in the linings of the bedrooms and some bees had broken through the wallpaper and this had been patched over with cardboard. There was no hot water and only one element on the top of the electric stove, functioned; and one element in the oven was working. The sheep yards would have been the envy of that famous Australian cartoonist named Joliffe, whose etching of Salt Bush Bill and the Aboriginal tribe Wichety of the Australian Outback that so amused his New Zealand and Australian readers.

I was later to take an Australian farmer friend from Albury, Victoria, who I had invited over to my youngest daughter's wedding up to the farm to see Old Fred's home-made sheep dip. In a slight dip in the land in his house paddock, a small spring had emerged and which trickled down the depression in the land over a papa (soft grey rock) outcrop before dropping down into a deep gorge. Fred had shaped this smooth, pliable rock into a trough to hold the water for the dip. A piece of old down pipe took care of the overflow. A number of flattened benzene tins, next to the dip acted as a draining board, then a make-shift race to let the dipped sheep out into the paddock. Upstream, where the small spring emerged from the ground, Fred had scooped out a small hole to let the water accumulate enough to mix the ingredients of the spray. The mixture then flowed downstream into the hewn papa dip and Fred was in business to dip his flock. Somewhat unhygienic, as the animals further down had to drink the water. Perhaps the old farmer depended on the waterfall into the gorge and the stream being in accessible for some distance, that nature's purification system would apply. Fred had some strange ideas about burglars; he claimed that someone had stolen his own bedroom and front door key, so he had inserted a slasher into the architrave to prevent anyone from opening the door. A padlock with no key was hooked onto a loose piece of chain and hooked onto a nail at the back door - this was supposed to deter any intruder. I mused to myself as I viewed this dilapidated spectacle of a home, what a wonderful experience for my youngest son who was crazy about sheep farming, to be able to rough it for a while as he had been so used to the large lovely home I had built myself for my seven children. When Mark, my youngest son, was occupying the old house on his first lambing beat, the lady on the farm next door said to him," Mark, do you mean to tell me you can put up with no hot water, little power and no TV., in that old house?" Mark's reply was music to my ears." " Lady," he replied, "All I want to hear is the rain on the roof!"

However, they were soon to fix that, they stole him from me with the oldest trick in the book! Being well trained to cope with disaster we just carried on without him.

The real nightmare of dealing with Fred, the owner, was only just beginning. He crutched and dagged his sheep right up until the last day before we took over. Mark used to go up and help him which the old farmer really appreciated. On the first day Mark helped him crutch, Old Fred had old, torn trousers on and three jerseys full of holes, that did not match except for one hole in the middle where a spark must have burnt through, as he slept by the open fire. Mark always dressed tidily with a decent warm bush shirt, plus warm corduroy trousers. Before they started crutching, Fred said, "Now for this job, you need really old clothes, so what the hell are you all dressed up for?"

I had by this time signed the bill of sale, but Fred had not because as usual, he was still an unwilling seller – he never really did want to leave the farm. Every time Fred visited the land agent, he changed the conditions of sale. He informed the agent that I would have to pay for the last years' top dressing spread, by a Dakota from the Napier airport. When I queried the request he replied, "Because you are going to get all the benefit!" Thinking how badly I wanted the property, I agreed. Then next he refused to pay his share of the rates, which are usually proportioned out to buyer and seller in accordance with the terms of takeover. Then one day, when I was up at the farm with the agent, Fred drew me aside and complained they were going to charge him so many thousand pounds commission. Of course, I had to sympathise with him to my regret, when I found the next time I visited the land agent to see if Fred had signed, Fred had added the commission to my price. Only the vision of all those flourishing rows of potatoes, all in flower and dams full of wild ducks, made me initial the new addition. The farm to us and what we wanted it for, was still a bargain, despite the addition and the state of the property, as it presented such a challenge. Next time Fred visited the agent, he queried him on how much longer was it going to take to clinch the deal! The agent relied, "Well, you have made so many changes and Jim has had to initial them all and you have to do the same." To which Fred immediately complied. "Now," said the agent, "To make all those initials legal, you have to sign it at the bottom." Fred did and at last we were in business and Fred could no longer back out or change anything. Even though I had complied with his demands, I knew we would never regret the extra cost as we had the trucks, the tractors, the manpower, the finances and the incentive of such a challenge to bring the property into full production.

Even though we were going to have to build over six miles of road, boundary and internal fences, a new woolshed, new cattle and sheep yards, new dip, 35 lakes and dams, new implement shed and hay shed and someday a new homestead. We just could not wait to start, it was such a challenge! With so much cash from the potato crop which was collateral to raise a $35,000 loan from the Rural bank, (who incidentally had been trying to get the old farmer off the property for years); and $2,000 from the Government Life Insurance company where myself and 4 sons all had life policies. But, alas, there was one more bombshell. Old Fred refused to sign the transfer unless I paid the last year's rates which of course were ridiculous! I got in touch with my solicitor, who informed me I did not have to pay them, but I would have to take him to the high court to occupy the property; and this of course would cause a lot of delay and expense. As lambing had already started, we needed access immediately, so once again I paid up, thinking, 'What's another $500, if we're going to own the farm!"

Then came the nightmare of getting the old guy off the property – he just did not want to leave! I had to be extremely diplomatic as I could see he was so upset at losing his farm. He actually cried when he left. I told him we wanted to renovate the house and at last he understood. It was partly true - we really had to tidy it up with a lot of new paint work outside and in, to brighten up such a dark interior. When I'd a fencer staying in the house with Mark and the opossums started playing 'ring a rosies' up in the ceiling, the fencer thought someone was trying to break in and used to shout out to the non-existent intruder to, "Get the hell out of it!".

I asked the fencer, "What on earth was Marks' reaction to all the commotion?" The fencer replied, "Oh, he just stopped snoring!" Actually Fred really did not need the money, he had thousands of dollars in the bank, and his accountant thought he was the best farmer in the district, apart from his rates and the one and only time he top dressed, his gross takings were his net profit. He shore all his own sheep himself and crutched the whole flock. When he had to dock the lambs, he employed several boys from town to catch the lambs for him. Fred had nine dogs, all with wires in their noses to stop biting, I suppose. Fred's dogs would hold a mob tightly in the corner of a paddock and the boys would work their way into the mob, grab a lamb and take it to Fred, who sat on a benzene box, tailed it, earmarked it, and removed the 'crown jewels' of any ram lamb. He never ever paid the boys any money. He kept several hives of bees, so he used to give each lad a tin of honey and say, 'Now this honey is your wages and you have to sell it on the way home, if you want any money!"

Fred ran quite a large number of turkeys on the farm and so wanting to cash in on his flock, before he left, he built an ingenious, long wire netting cage. He drove all the birds into the cage to catch them, so as not to panic the whole mob which could have easily flown away.

He also rang his neighbour, Jock Elliot, to ask if he could come over to Jock's farm and pick up his turkeys which had strayed on to his place. Jock, being an amiable, friendly man of a kindly disposition, granted his permission. However, on thinking about his own turkeys, he rang Fred back and asked him how many turkeys did he think he had on Jock's farm to pick up?

"Why the lot of course," replied Fred. "But what about the turkeys that have bred on my place?" queried Jock.

"They all came from my eggs," replied Fred.

Permission was naturally withdrawn, simply because there was an unwritten law or understanding between farmers, that whoever's farm a mob of turkeys was in, belonged to that farm, as the mobs wandered and bred from farm to farm. There was no possible way of really establishing who the mob belonged to, as the birds were always moving about to where the best grass was. The only time he ever paid for any help, was in his last year of owning the farm and his bad leg was giving him trouble. He employed two Maori shearers to help him shear his flock. However, poor Fred was so difficult to get on with; he had a row with them, told them to come to his house and paid them off. While writing out the two cheques, he noticed one of the shearers took off, but later reappeared. Fred thought that was strange and later found out why. When the shearers finally left, Fred went over to carry on the shearing by himself. He went to start up his old Lister engine that drove the shearing plant, it coughed and spluttered and after a few misfires, stopped altogether. Fred, thinking it was out of petrol, peered into the tank, only to find out that it had been filled with sheep droppings! When we were shifting Fred and loading all of his belongings onto our big flat deck truck, parked at the front door, my son Barry came across a huge preserving jar filled with strange looking liquid placed on Fred's mantle piece. Fred had saved the contents of the petrol tank and that was when he told us all of his strange stories. It was a tough job sorting out Fred's belongings of what he wanted to take with him when he left because Fred never threw anything away – waste not want not, was his mantra! He even saved all the turkey claws and had them tied up in little bundles in his shed. Also the shed was stacked to the roof with newspapers and he complained that he would have to go through them all to see why he kept them. Even though Fred had been such a pain all though the transaction, I still felt sorry for him, as his wife and family had all left him and he seemed such a lonely man who had to finally give up his home and farm. He told Mark one day,

" You know what I like most about your family? You boys get on well with your father!" He also informed him that, "In all the negotiations, your father was good, but Tilley (that was the name of the agent), he made me sign the bill of sale without my glasses!"

That was how close it came to not being sold!

Fred tried to sell me most of his furniture while we were loading his belongings into our truck. I bought his large living room table, which was heart rimu, and several antique chairs, thinking they would be handy for the staff when we would be harvesting potatoes. He was delighted when I offered him 10 pounds. But the sofa? "Oh no, Fred, I have a sofa."

"Ok," he said, "You've got a sofa, but put it on the truck."

As we lifted the sofa up, we heard a whole lot of walnuts (there was huge walnut tree near the house), rattle down to one end. When we tipped the sofa the other way onto the deck of the truck, all the walnut shells, plus a lot of mutton bones, fell out of a hole in the end where the rats had hoarded them after Fred had finished his dinner by the open fire!

Finally after a lot of sorting, loading and so little discarding, we had the truck loaded, all except the odd items that Fred claimed were secret and took them into his bedroom. He actually cried when we were about to leave.

"Take my farm would you!" he muttered.

However, there was more hassle to come, by a strange act of fate or destiny. Fred found out that through all the documentation, that he knew my accountant. He had acted for him in, when working in a firm that handled his divorce. Fred could not believe his luck. With nothing better to do when he retired to the city, he kept calling on my accountant claiming he still had not been paid for everything. He had a long list on a narrow piece of paper.

There were 4 steers in the big scrub he had failed to muster, some harrows, a bucket of precious stones and many other items. The only way I could stop these visits to my accountant was to tell him to charge Fred, not me for his time. Also to tell Fred, he was welcome to come and pick up his steers and oddments anytime he wished.

At last it all came to an end and we were free of his hassles once he learned it was going to cost him. Our first job was to tackle over 6 miles of fencing, which had to be renewed; to build new cattle and sheep yards and build a new wool shed in a better location. There was a large pinus radiata forest from the front gate into the old house site, so having all the gear we felled a large number of these well matured trees, transported them on our largest truck to a nearby timber mill. We then carted the milled timber down to the city to be tantalised. It was a huge operation as we had to mill enough timber for a 4 stand woolshed, a new house and a hay barn as well as an implement shed. During the next two years, we built 35 dams and ponds, a lot of the streams that ran through the farm were in gorges and so inaccessible to stock. At times we had two bulldozers crushing scrub and kanuka and building dams. The potatoes we produced in the rich volcanic loam were of the finest quality. Some days, we had two seven ton trucks filled by 2pm, which was not too bad in those days when potatoes harvesters were only new to the industry. We had to concrete two crossings over the stream to the paddocks that were previously inaccessible. For ten years, we ploughed all the income from the farm, market garden and orchard, back into the farm to improve and bring the land into full production. I certainly got more pleasure and satisfaction out of spending so much money than Fred did out of saving all his pounds. Even though Fred may have been just a little over cautious in spending money, you cannot condemn a person for saving, there is just not enough of it done these days. I had a wonderful mother who taught me how to save even when I was quite young. There was no such thing as an allowance or pocket money, when I was a lad. You had to earn every penny by doing odd jobs for people, mushrooming or blackberrying. I was only twelve years old when I decided to fill a twelve pound tomato box of blackberries and take it to the local auction market. When the store man lifted the lid so the berries could be viewed and auctioned, the buyers all gasped. No one had ever thought of selling such berries, they were generally looked upon as a picnic food, taken out to the local riverbed which was covered with such bushes. This was a day the whole family filled billies of blackberries all to be made into pies and jam.

"Here's a real novelty!" cried the auctioneer.

The buyers and onlookers were amazed when the berries were sold for 61/2 pence per pound to a city hotel. It was the 1930's, slump time. Money was tight, so on the weekend, everyone was out picking blackberries and the price dropped to 3 pence per pound, but from that time onwards, blackberries were a part of every sale - they never did reach the sixpence ½ pence per pound again. Supply had exceeded demand. When I started my first permanent job in 1934 at one pound per week, mother said she would only charge me 10 shillings a week for my board, if I banked the remaining ten shillings in my Post Office Savings Account, I readily accepted and have her to thank for the financial position I am in today. In those days I still had a small garden, plus weekend work in a market garden to buy my clothes, ammunition for deer stalking, pig hunting and duck shooting. These helped put food on the table during those hard times of the 1930's depression.

I used to give sound economic advice to all the young lads that helped with the harvest on the weekends and school holidays. It would have been the first time they had ever had a decent amount of money to handle, so I used to advise them not to buy a flash motorbike or an old bomb of a car as that would keep them poor, but rather save it all and invest it. A big ask of lads so young. I know in such affluent times when everyone was in a spend, spend, spend mood. However, some took heed. One such lad used to lend his older brother ten shillings, so he could take his girlfriend to the movies; he was charged 2 shillings a week interest! The family used to call the lender, Scrooge Mc Duck. But he was misnamed – he was a good business man who listened to his tutor. I used to tell the boys to stash their earning away, and then buy an old house, full of wood worm; someday you will pull it down, sell the section, and more than triple your money. The lad they called Scrooge is now in business in Australia and I will wager he is close to being a millionaire!

It is strange how some people think. A few people I talked to exclaimed,

What a crazy time it was to be buying a farm!"

Lamb was only fetching four dollars a head. I tried to explain it was not only the right time to buy when prices hit rock bottom, but the only time I could afford to! It was not long before fat lambs rose to eight dollars, then fourteen, then twenty four, forty five and today two hundred dollars a head – that's inflation for you. Only a few years ago after we had bought the farm, a neighbouring farm sold for the unheard of price of three hundred and six dollars per acre, the vendor could not believe it. At the time a very conservative government was in power, with a tax and prime minister who put the country's sixty million sheep on social security to encourage reproduction. The farming industry became fully subsidised, there were supplementary meat payments, subsidised stock drenches, fertilizers and even top dressing by plane. Farming boomed, young farmers bought into property at inflated prices, sixty million sheep became seventy million in a market that was oversupplied. Then a socialist government was elected who did not appreciate the importance of the contribution the farming industry made to the economy in the propping up of the welfare state. They wiped all the subsidies and so doing, destroyed any equity young farmers had invested in over priced farms as farm prices dropped drastically. The new government imposed a sales tax on every purchase including rates, which was already a kind of tax. Consequently the value of farms took a steep dive, but only for two years. As farmers came back down to earth from all the previous artificial prosperity and reality took over, returns began to improve and the next thing we knew the dairy industry took off and ever since sheep numbers have dropped to an all time low of about twelve million with so many sheep properties being converted to dairying; in fact if it was not for dairy produce, lumber and beef, we would become a typical banana republic. Perhaps I should have added tourism to the list.

The day after we took over the farm, my youngest son Mark, and I began dismantling a dilapidated fence, close to the road, when a local farmer pulled up and on approaching us, enquired, "Has this property really been sold?"

I replied, "Well, we would not be able to dismantle this apology for a fence if it had not".

"I suppose not," He answered, "How on earth did you do it? I have been trying to buy this farm for years, like most of the other neighbours."

"Well," I answered, "After a great deal of hassling and living alongside Mason Waterworth and Lew Harris for 30 years, old Fred was a piece of cake!"

Mason and Lew were extremely astute farmers and property investors, who purchased farms, at the very bottom of the trough in a downturn in business. One day later when some of the local farmers were discussing my purchase and all the extras Fred had imposed on the deal; and that it was folly for me to have paid them, when one of the farmers interrupted and said,

"Hang on a minute, but Jim got the farm!"

They all looked at each other and laughed saying, "That's right, he did!"

I do not think that John Maynard Keynes would have given old Fred many points for the results of his economic prowess, but I am sure he would have received full marks for trying.

There was a small mob of red deer on the farm at the time of purchase. A big stag with five hinds. Local farm hands, rabbiters and the like, had tried to shoot the stag for years as the animal had a magnificent head, but it was too cunning as farm stags usually are. One poacher, took a single, shot at it one day near the road, but missed and Old Fred came driving down the road in a panic to apprehend the poacher, asking the man who had just fired the shot, if he had seen anybody?

"No," replied the poacher. "I'll help you look for him."

After we had taken over the farm, we began crushing huge tracts of heavy kanuka and bracken fern, opening up previously; inaccessible areas where the big red deer stag and his five hinds lived. Farm hands, rabbiters and meat hunters had tried for years to hunt down the stag for its magnificent head of antlers, but the stag had eluded them all. My son, Mark, when riding his horse around the farm used to sometimes come across the stag grazing in a clearing and it would just trot away looking back at him, such animals know when they're not being hunted. Although I did not want the small mob of deer shot, as I thought it was great to have a farm with deer on it. I realised that clearing the heavy kanuka, I would be destroying their habitat, so I left large areas in ravines, gorges and steep hillsides in their natural form. The native bush of Five Fingers, Supple Jack, Thousand Jacket, young Rimus, young Kahikatea, Rewarewa, Clematis and huge tree ferns, were all too magnificent to destroy. They also gave sanctuary for the deer to retreat into. However, the natural habitat I provided was still not enough. At the time of crushing large tracts of tall kanuka, on quiet gentle slopes and renewing old fences, I had two young neighbours as contract fencers working on a road fence line and another young man, a shepherd, on a neighbour's property, building a new road fence further up the highway. Another neighbour named Gary Christensen, who owned a property on my southern boundary and who had worked for me thinning lettuces in my market garden when he was at high school, helped my son, Mark with all the sheep work like lambing, docking and shearing.

One morning when Gary and I were walking on the edge of a large kanuka scrub block, that was next to be crushed, we noticed unusual footprints in the giant discing that clearly showed distinct hobnail boot marks in the freshly turned over volcanic soil. Following the footprints towards the forest, we found the entrails of a deer that had recently been shot. On examination, Gary, an experienced deerstalker, exclaimed, "Why it's the stag!"

"How do you know?" I asked.

Gary replied, "Look at the size of its heart."

We looked at each other in dismay; we both knew we had three deer meat hunters building fences on the property. I straight away thought that it was David the fencer working on his own. He was a good worker, but a bit of a character in more ways than one. Gary did not think David would take the risk and jeopardize his contract. When I went home that night and told my wife, an extremely intelligent lady, she agreed with me. The question was how to find out. Next morning, while talking to David, I got around to the deer being shot and David asked,

"Has there been a deer shot on your property?"

When I answered that there had, he said that he was going into town that afternoon as there is only one place you can sell the meat. He would find it for me. When he arrived back, he informed me, that there had been nothing taken in to be sold all week. He then asked me if I would like to give him a hand to staple the new roadside fence he was erecting. I willingly agreed. He gave me an apron of concrete post staples and said,

"I'll go ahead and staple the hollows – you follow me and staple the rises."

So off we went stapling. It so happened that the fence line had to be bulldozed to clear all the scrub, blackberry and bracken fern to enable the fence to be built. On following David, I immediately noticed David's boot marks were of hobnails. My boots, Gary's and all the other boys wore rubber soled boots. I was right. The imprints could only have been David's. How on earth was I going to get David to own up? It turned out to be easy. We had finished stapling and David had begun work on a new line. Meanwhile Gary had been driving down the road to where John and Alan were fencing. Gary pulled up, he knew John and Alan really well, and all three were well thought of in the district. Gary approached the two and said, "Now look here, you guys. I want an honest answer. Did you or did you not shoot Jim's stag?"

John and Alan looked at each other in dismay. "No, we never shot his flipping stag, but we know who did!"

'Who, then?" asked Gary. "Why David, he's got the head hanging up in his shed, he showed it to us. He said he had shot it in Bob Peddle's scrub and that Bob had taken a shot at him as he carried it out."

The crux of the situation was of course, that David wanted to enter such a magnificent head of antlers in the Kawekas Deerstalkers Annual Competition and he had to have an alibi for where he had shot it.

"Come down and relate the incident to Jim," pleaded Gary.

I was down at the gate where David's fence line started and was working on some new rails. I had a big Pontiac car at the time, so after John and Alan related their surprising story, I said,

"Hop in the back!"

Gary got in the front and we drove up to where David was ramming a new post in. He took one look at who was in the back seat and knew the game was up. I got out and said.

"Well, David, we have some more deerstalking to discuss!"

In a very quiet voice he said, "Yes, I shot your stag."

John and Alan complained they did not jump out of the car quickly enough to hear the confession. David looked downfallen and said,

"I suppose you will want all the money ($400.00) I got for the meat?"

I said, "No, you can keep the money, but I want the head!"

I had the head mounted and it is hanging on the wall in my front entrance hallway of my home to this day. David pleaded with me to enter the head in the deerstalkers competition and as joint entry. However, I was so upset at the stag being shot, I refused. The stag had eluded so many hunters for so long; David thought he had achieved the ultimate in deerstalking. What had happened was as it was summertime, with long evenings of daylight, David and I would work until almost 8.00pm, then I went home. David had gone back to the paddock where the stag had just come out to feed. He shot but only wounded the animal and it had run up into the tall scrub block and died where we found the remains. I had a close friend who lived on his father's farm at Puketitiri and they had a pet deer hind which one day was grazing in their front roadside paddock. Some deerstalkers spotted it as they were passing shot at the animal. They should have known it was a pet as it was not only grazing with the farm stock, but did not run when the hunter's vehicle stopped. There were two kinds of hunters – one category observes the rules and there are poachers, who even shoot farm stock and thus give the recreation a bad name. My friend informed me that these hunters who shot their pet deer only wounded it and the animal was able to make its way back to the farmhouse for sanctuary. But it was severely wounded and it died in my friend's sister's arms as she tried to comfort her pet. A truly genuine hunter is always a conservationist. With all the ponds and dam we built, we only shot on a few of them – the rest were a sanctuary. We transported huge loads of raupo from a neighbours swamp with two big tip trucks and unloaded it into the deepest end of the small lakes where it flourished and provided safe cover for young ducklings and chicks in the breeding season. With such a safe habitat, all kinds of waders and swamp bird made it their home. There were rails, grebes, herons, swamp hens and recently pair of black swan, (an indigenous bird to Australia and New Zealand) who have had a clutch of four this year, five cygnets in the last few years. Even though the swans are included in our shooting licence, I would not dream of taking any of these birds, even if they increase dramatically, as it is such a privilege and an achievement, to have them breed on my property. Because the birds know they are safe as we constantly view their activities and young cygnets, they become unwary and are therefore prone to poachers. After I lost the big stag, his hinds were shot one by one until the whole mob was exterminated. For some years there were no deer on this property, however a few years ago, a farmer downstream of our creek, with over thousand areas of heavy scrub, which was the habitat of over 30 deer, began clearing large tracts of the forest. This man's father Bob Peddle, a very close friend of mine, even though a duck shooter, was a great conservationist and never, ever allowed any of his deer to be taken. He and his family used to love to see them on a summer evening walking past the house on their way over to this immense scrub block. Bob's son,

Gary, following in his father's footsteps, is also a strong conservationist and never allows any deerstalking on his property; although many poachers tried to trespass the deer's habitat. When Gary began clearing some of the easier contours of the scrub block, it forced some of the deer upstream onto my property where there was still ample cover of large tracts of thick and heavy kanuka. Wild deer know they are a hunted animal and therefore have to have plenty of cover to hide and breed in. My main helper, Wally Allen and I have observed small lots of four deer and I have often seen small mobs come down to drink at our largest pond. Of course with the deer coming back to our farm, poachers, always aware of any deer movements, are on the prowl again and quite recently, Wally found the head of a spiker, that is a one year old stag, with just two horns, thrown into a blackberry bush, which had been sprayed, but since died, revealing the evidence of poachers being active once more.

Two years ago, the turkeys on the farm had a great breeding season and the mob increased to 30 birds. However, poachers took the lot so now there is not one turkey in the farm. In the past, Wally and I took only four turkeys each year, one each for Christmas dinner and two for friends for the same purpose. Most rabbiters, and some farmhands and some possum trappers are well known for their poaching activities and are difficult to apprehend, especially the professional poachers who have been known to take even farm stock. Quite recently, there has been a spate of thefts of farm animals being stolen off farms at night. A friend of mine had 45 sheep slaughtered one night; however, they caught the culprits. Three years ago, a pair of black swans flew into one of our dams that were well covered in natural flora around the edges. They were evidently looking for a nesting site and choose a well covered dam for this purpose, so predatory hawks could not molest their young cygnets. This pair of swans brought up their clutches of cygnets the last two years. However, they got so used to our presence they became easy prey for poachers who recently shot the lot, including the five cygnets from a second hatching. That is the trouble with poachers – they are not conservationists, they exterminate everything they can!

*One of the larger lakes that we built out of the wilderness that
provides a habitat for swans, mallard ducks, grebes, herons,
swamp hens (pukeko), kingfishes and cormorants*

The most amazing thing about Fred's farm was its lack of drinking
water for the stock. Not a single water trough or dam existed. The
stream was only partly available as most of it ran through gorges and
was therefore inaccessible. Most of Fred's internal fences traversed down
through the middle of wet gullies as stock couldn't get access from either
side of any spring water that may be available, although these gullies
were littered with the remains of bogged animals searching for water in
drought conditions. If Fred had only realised the price of the lost cattle
would have paid for all the dams he needed. Our first task of course was
the availability of good water. We built a dam in the house paddock as
soon as we took over. It filled up in four days from a good spring and
supplied three paddocks. That was the most wonderful aspect of the
farm; almost every gully had a strong spring we could tap. As we built
dam after dam, and they all filled rapidly with lovely, clean water, we
were able to stock the farm with increasing numbers of cattle. If there
was one thing cattle must have in the heat of summer, it is access to good
water and plenty of shade. The more dams we built the more we could
subdivide into smaller paddocks and increase our stock rates.

Our inquisitive, friendly steers on the farm,
always wondering what we were up to.

In conclusion to the explanation of this unusual transaction with such a strange vendor and who probably thought the same of me, I can only calculate that I learnt still more about human nature and how it simply defies analysis. The head of the Rural Bank later informed me that they had been trying to get the old farmer off his property for years as it was the only farm in the area that had not been broken in and was unproductive. He too, was amazed that the agent had finally succeeded after so many had failed. Perhaps it was just due to timing more than anything. It was such triumph for the agent that he put on a special dinner for my whole family, including my married children and my accountant and his wife.

GOOD NEIGHBOURS

Chapter 5

During the nineteenth century when the province of Hawkes Bay was being settled and the first school and churches were being built, the Catholic priests established their church on a low lying farming district called Meeanee. In the early days, the three rivers that traversed the Heretaunga Plains flooded all the low lying areas as at that time their flows were not contained by the stop banks or levies. However, in the Meeanee district, the constant flooding had enforced the local settlers to build their homes on extra high wooden piles or blocks, so that the persistent floodwaters would flow well under the floor boards of their houses. The flood waters would be about one foot high as they had such a vast area of low lying land to cover. In 1897, the province experienced the most disastrous flood of all, when the water was almost a huge sheet from Napier South to nearly Hastings. From then on stop banks began to be built to try and contain the rivers flow in times of heavy rain. However, these stop banks often gave way and the flood waters still would cover the whole of the low lying areas. Most of the settlers were dairy farmers and when the rivers began rising they would open their farm gates and let their whole herd out to wander up to the higher ground, around the village of Taradale which was not prone to flooding and situated near the foothills. As a young boy I lived in a street that was near these hills. I would awake up in the morning of a big flood to the sound of several herds of dairy cows all mooing loudly as they grazed on the luscious grass in our street. I used to ask my mother why they were making so much noise and she informed me they all wanted to be milked. One farmer owned a 36 acre block in the local hills where I have been growing crops for the last 72 years. He used this as a run—off for any of his dry cattle, but he informed me that at flood times and he let his animals out for safety, they would go straight up to this hill block and he would travel up the next morning to let them into this safe haven. There they would be quietly grazing the roadside outside the properties main gate, waiting to be let in. It never ceased to amaze me how all these small herds never ever got mixed up. When the flood waters receded, off they would go, sometimes with the help of the owners of course, bulls and cows to their respective farms. I was to find out why much later in life when I farmed cattle. I would purchase different lots of 18 month steers, say ten, twelve, fourteen and they seldom mixed. They would all come over to feed when I fed out the hay but the different small mobs would go off on their own when the hay was finished. I once purchased a dozen steers from the Chatham Islands and they would not even feed with the whole mob when I fed out. They just stood off and watched, then cautiously approached when I moved away.

It so turned out that the 1897 flood was so disastrous, that the Catholic priests decided to shift their constantly flooded vineyard to a safe hillside site situated on an excellent block of undulating slopes on the Greenmeadows hills. The farm of over 500 acres was ideal for grapes and stock farming. They also built a large two storied seminary that housed one hundred young students who were to be trained as brothers and priests. A beautiful stone church was also erected, but unfortunately this church collapsed in the 1931 earthquake, taking the lives of several young priests. The whole complex was known as Mount St Mary's Mission. The wines it produced won many gold medals and made a great name for its brand both in New Zealand and overseas. It so happened that the Mission farm bordered just across the road of the southern boundary of the property where I resided and produced fruit and vegetables for the New Zealand market. We also had several blocks on the alluvial plain in different areas where we produced large quantities of main crop and early potatoes, cauliflower, cabbage, lettuce and tomatoes.

One day two gentlemen from the Mission called into one of these vegetable blocks and enquired of one of my sons, as to the possibility of purchasing any second grade vegetables we may have available. My son informed them that his father would not charge them for second grade produce and that they could have as much as we had available for free. The Brothers, as that was what the young helpers at the Mission were known as, insisted they wanted to pay for the produce. However, my son emphasised that I would not accept any money and that I would be glad to have someone to be able to use it as it was too good to waste. The Brothers then enquired if I would like some wine in remuneration to which my son replied, "But my father doesn't drink."

When my son told me of the incident, I laughed to myself but did not let on I would have loved a bottle of wine! I did not drink because I could not afford too. I not only had seven children, but several mortgages, a decent overdraft, as we were buying tractors, trucks and other machinery. Alcohol was furthest from my thoughts and beside I wanted to set an example to my children. So quite sizeable quantities of slightly under grade top quality vegetables were delivered to the Mission's kitchen for which they were most grateful. Then one day, the two Brothers that had negotiated the arrangement with, called at my pack house with a long list of all the produce they had received, wanting to pay me for it. "No, No", I insisted, "you are most welcome; there is no need for payment."

They seemed quite embarrassed and kept on insisting that they would at least like to pay for something. However, I refused to accept their offer and finally said, "Look, if you are so determined to reward me for it all, you have something over the road on your farm that is worth more than all the money in the world to me." They looked at each other and then to me in astonishment. "What on earth is it?" they queried.

"Some dams I could take my boys over to after a hard day's work, to shoot a few ducks."

"Is that all?" they replied, "We'll see what we can do."

Apparently everything like this comes up, a meeting is called at the seminary to discuss and vote on the matter. When the two brothers explained the request, Brother Sylvester, the head in charge of running the seminary, exclaimed in a loud voice, "Give him the lot!" Such was their appreciation or our contribution to their requirements. However, one of the Brothers who worked in the vineyard and kept the birds from consuming the grapes, was an excellent shot and claimed he liked to have a shot at the ducks too. But Brother Sylvester spoke against this request saying, "You only ever come home with one duck. What is the use of one duck among 100 students and besides we are not supposed to consume such rich fare" When the two Brother informed me of all this, I replied that we didn't need all we shot and that just a few choice ones would be ample. We wouldn't want to deprive anyone of their pastime and besides, you folk should have the richest food available with all the good you do". One of my sons even prepared a hide on a dam and shot with the Brother who had objected. A few days after the season opened, Brother Sylvester concerned that we should do well in the shooting, enquired of me when I was delivering some vegetables, "Tell me Mr Clayton, how did you get on with the ducks?" "Well, I said, "It's hard to believe, but we had swarms of duck frequenting the dams before the opening, but when we were sitting in our hides, the first night in great anticipation, the first mob came over a bit too early, flew around and around several times out of range, then settled on top of the hill above the dam and had a discussion about the situation, listened to ascertain if there were any live birds on the water, took a vote, deciding the still in the water decoys were phoney and flew back to the sanctuary from whence they had come."

"Ah, well, Mr Clayton," Brother Sylvester replied," you must realise that God is on the side of the ducks!" "How right you are," I replied. However, I did relieve his anxiety when I informed him that we did well out of the later flights. From then on he always tried to make it up with a case of wine, four of his best Ports, four Sherries and four Sauterne; such was his appreciation of all our produce.

Over the years the intake of one hundred students gradually decreased until there was only one, then not any at all. This magnificent site and buildings have now been turned into a very popular restaurant. I think it is very sad such a wonderful seminary, that trained so many priests and brothers had to close because of the lack of entrants. I miss the students, who used to come up to our new potato blocks every Wednesday when they had the afternoon off, to follow the potato digger picking up all the seconds and little ones, which they so enjoyed for their own consumption. I also went to visit the Mission on odd evenings to instruct them on vegetable production as they had a large garden but little knowledge of what to grow. I always emphasised the importance of maintaining a healthy soil structure if you wanted to produce nutritious health giving vegetables. I gave the young priests a fertiliser distributer to help them out make their efforts a lot easier. It all must have been absorbed because some years later received a letter from a Father Mc Very, who had been ordained and sent to the Island of Buma off the coast of the Solomon's. He enclosed in his letter some New Zealand dollars for me to purchase some seeds for him as he had 300 odd children to look after and feed. He informed me that they were going to lose their overseas supply of food. Their small area of productive land was impoverished and hardly enough to feed his charges, so he wanted to know what to grow. I wrote back and informed him to gather as much seaweed as he could, to work into their small area of land to try and build up the soil fertility. He wrote back to say that seaweed did not grow in the tropics. I therefore informed him to gather all the leaf mould from the jungle to spread over their garden to help improve the soil structure which would increase the yield of their sweet potato crop. I never heard back so still wonder how they survived.

I related these experiences I had with such a great bunch of young students, a hundred all told, all training to be priest and now not any and can only wonder in such a changing world, if there are not so many coming forward to continue such vital work. My association with the seminary even allowed me to play a small part in saving one of their parishioner's life. I had a retired farmer helping me on the land and one day he seemed unusually quiet and withdrawn. As we were always close friends, I enquired of him, "You seem pretty quiet and subdued today, Jack, is there anything wrong?"

"Yes, yes," he replied. "Jill (not her real name) is going to take her own life."

His niece had family problems and it seemed she could no longer cope. "Has she talked to her priest?" I enquired. "No, she will not have anything to do with him." He replied. "That's a pity." I said. He paused for a while, and then said, "You are pretty chummy with all those chaps up at the Mission, how about having a yarn to one of them?" "All right," I said. "If you think it will help. The trouble was I knew so many but did not know who would be the best to approach on such an urgent problem. I decided to enquire from the farm manager who would be best. 'One of our parishioners is going to take her life, I informed him. "can you tell me whom would be the best to see up at the seminary to help her?" he thought for a while, then said," See father Sloane". I immediately did and explained the situation how the lady concerned could not approach the local priest. Father Sloane just nodded and said, "Yes, I understand, he can be difficult. Leave it to me." He thanked me and a life was saved! The lady concerned (who I did not even know) married again and lived, I am sure, a much happier life. It was however, not really Jack or I that saved that lady. It was a Devine action and a classic example of just how God works. God engaged Jack, a Presbyterian, to approach myself, and Anglican, to seek the advice of the farm manager, a Catholic, as to who would be the best priest to consult over such a delicate and urgent matter. It was also a great example of how different denominations can work together. The Mission were always so grateful for all our produce, they always seemed as if they wanted to reimburse us still further and often gave us smallgoods like sausages and savaloys, made by Brother Leo, who produced these delicacies as he was the kitchen butcher. One day when I was delivering vegetables and I had empty vegetables crates to pick up, Brother Sylvester wanted to give me another carton of wine and was organising who would help me with the crates, he said, "Perhaps it would be better if Brother Aubyn to go down with Brother Clayton – Oh, I do beg your pardon, Mr Clayton. I do apologize!" I was, from then on, an honorary "Brother Clayton".

During the 1970's when my wife and I were in British Columbia in Canada, visiting an apple orchard, I noticed a monument erected to a Father Mendosi of France, who had planted the first apple trees there and so started the apple industry. I wrote to Brother Sylvester informing him of such an interesting incident and signed myself "Brother Clayton". He was so pleased to hear from me, he pinned my letter up on a notice board at the college. When a new priest, who did not know me, read the letter, he enquired, who on earth was this Bother Clayton. Brother Sylvester explained, "He is our representative at Expo '70 in Japan and if you ever get to do the same good deeds he has achieved, you might too might be similarly rewarded." Brother Sylvester informed me that when the new priest found out whom I really was, his weights really dropped. He had begun his letter by saying, Dear Mr and Mrs Clayton, or should I say Brother and Sister Clayton..." I have that letter to this very day and really treasure it.

One thing I am certain of is that Mount st Mary's Mission could not have found anyone better to manage such a seminary than Brother Sylvester. Although he had a great sense of humour, he was most strict on discipline. He ran a tight, economical ship and was respected by everyone. My family missed the students when it finally closed, they were the best – I suppose they had to be, for the calling they had chosen. I used to ring the Mission every Wednesday morning and inform them which block of potatoes we would be digging, so the students could come up and follow the digger, picking o the little potatoes as they had Wednesday afternoon off. When they had picked up enough for their needs, they used to come over and thank me and then offer to help us. They were so grateful.

The Mission always seemed to think that the three weeks season we had duck shooting on their farm was insufficient reward for all the produce we supplied to them, so they were always trying to find extra thinks to give us,

One day, several students brought up some huge preserving jars full of fig jam and said to my wife, "We believe you love fig jam". "I don't, "my wife replied, "But my husband does, it's his favourite."

'Oh my goodness," they replied, "well keep it all anyway." And if there is too much, just chuck it away as we have too much of it". And they all laughed. Apparently, the Mission had big trees and the cook had made too much fig jam and the students had been unable to absorb such a huge quantity. I was having a chat to a young Fijian student, one day and I asked how if they ever had periods of silence like in some other monasteries and he replied, "Oh no, perhaps only when we rise in the morning, we go about our duties not saying much. But I think that may be only because someone might have got up on the other side of the bed." When he saw me laughing, he laughed too, but I am sure he did not known what I was laughing at.

It was a sad day when the seminary finally closed and the intake of students, which was once a hundred, was reduced to one trainee.

They also decided to cease farming operations, but kept the vineyard and the winery operating. They put the farm up for lease by tender. So ended a long, happy relationship with a Good Neighbour.

It looked like the end of the duck shooting rights for me as I did not know the person who won the lease. However, I thought no harm in giving him a ring. When I explained I had been shooting there for 40 years and would it be possible to retain just one dam – the nearest to my boundary, he surprised by saying, "I don't see why not."

We have become close friends and he even began buying the best kind of cattle for my farm and sold them for me at the right time. I was so pleased with the returns, I promised to lease him the farm, if I could no longer manage it. He has now been leasing it for several years and has the property in tip top shape with wonderful pastures of red clover, white clover and Lotus Major – a yellow flowered native clover.

Bill Hoffman is his name and he and his wife, Jenny are among my closest friends. While family are most important, there is nothing quite as precious as true friends. They seek no ownership or reward; they are there for you when most needed. Their strength and support cannot be measured; their presence alone makes life worth living. Relations always seem to be competing for power or favours or money when the will is being read.

A wealthy business man up north left 50million dollars to his relatives and 50 million to a charity. "Not enough," said the relatives, and contested the charity's share.

A lawyer once told me he only needed to work two days a week to make a good living, with relatives fighting and contesting wills. My brother-in-law gave me examples of both his side of the family scrapping over money. He summed up life as being far happier if you are poor and have nothing to fight over. Sad, but perhaps true.

The movie starring, Kirk Douglas in 'Greedy', portrayed a very sad side of humanity as well as a kind of measure, the entire scenes being so well acted. Money does not have to be a curse -it is how you handle it that counts.

As I have already quoted, "the best things in life are still free; it's just that it takes an awful lot of money to sustain them.

THE AMAZING INTELLIGENCE
OF ALL LIVING THINGS

Chapter 6

While the human brain being so powerful has allowed mankind to dominate the earth and bring all other forms of life under its control, the extraordinary intelligence of tiny insects to the magnificent elephant is often not appreciated by mankind.

How often do we hear people saying of certain humans acting like "animals"? What a horrible thing it say about animals – that they were like humans! Animals may be a trifle primitive in their ablutions, but they live far better, normal lives than humanity. Mankind totally underestimates their intelligence. How often do we hear of someone being called a 'bird brain' or "as silly as a rabbit'?

I have often watched with amusement, a rabbit outwitting the craftiest of hunting dogs. As for birds, the following is a classic example of how such a small brain of a bird can overcome an obstacle.

In my orchard property, where we have many apricot trees which make ideal nesting sites for the many pairs of chaffinches that occupy our orchard. A pair of these birds had their nest blown away by an unusual storm. As the mother chaffinch was about to lay her eggs, a rebuilding programme was of urgent priority. When the nest was finished, my son was thinning the fruit and had observed all the construction haste, came over to me and said, "Dad, you will not believe this so you had better come over and see for yourself what these two birds have done to overcome the gales." This pair of chaffinches had flown down into our fertiliser shed and searched for a synthetic manure bag and pulled a length of tough material from the sack, woven it into their nest and then tied it to a twig so that no gale could dislodge it.

Pairs of fantails on our property always build their nests and hatch their young to coincide the exact time the fruit is ripe. Fantails are not a fruit eating bird – they live on insects like flies. They know that when the fruit is ripe, other birds peck the fruit which attracts the flies; hence dinner is served as the chicks are hatched. But it is the timing of the whole operation of the different maturing dates of the varieties that is so amazing. I once observed a little fantail sitting on her nest high up in a plum tree. It was a wet summer and the rain was emptying down and this poor little bird was trying to keep her eggs dry. I had a walnut tree growing nearby, so I procured some of it's big leaves and built a roof over the fantails nest to keep it dry. The mother fantail had got so used to seeing me thinning near her, that she never even flew away; she just looked up at the roof I had built. Yet another fantail upon a nest in the apricots, where my son was thinning, acted quite differently. He invited me up the ladder to view the work of art the fantail had created and said, "She will not fly away, she must have young ones". However, when the little bird saw me, a total stranger, she flew off the nest revealing four little cream eggs with brown spots. The fantail had got used to my son thinning near her nest, but I was a total stranger, so she took flight. A spider will often throw a web around a brunch of grapes knowing that a bird is going to peck them and so attract the flies, hence the spiders lunch, provided the fantail does not come along and consume both the spider and the flies of an 'a al carte' luncheon.

*A Californian Quai nest that was built by the pair, under
a wooden fruit pellet which was covered with boxes*

The intelligence of Californian Quail never ceases to amaze me. These
birds used to build their nest in my rows of early pumpkins, which had
rows of baled hay to protect the vines from wind. The quail used to pull
the straw out of the bales to build their nests and sometimes a pumpkin
would form and mature right alongside the nest, so I would have to leave
it until the chicks had hatched before I could harvest it.

In a particular wet season, mother quail must have said to her mate,"
I do not fancy sitting out there in Jim's pumpkins trying to keep my
eggs dry in all the rain! "What do you propose doing?" her mate would
have queried. "Let's have a look at Jim's sheds", she would have replied;
"Too easy for Jim's cat to catch the chicks!" her hubby would have said.
"I'll soon fix that!" the mother quail would reply. So she built a lovely
nest under the fruit pallet stacked with bushels cases on top of it. I
would never have found it had I not chased a young rabbit that was
eating my cauliflowers plants. It ran into the boxes on the pallet. I took
every box off the pallet but no rabbit! "Ah," I said to myself, "you are
under the pallet." So I lifted up the pallet and out flew mother quail
with a lovely nest of 12 eggs. I put everything back just as it was and
she went back and brought out 12 little chicks. Sometimes the quail

would nest in my petunias bed close to the back door, right under the nose of the cat, who always hunted afar, not dreaming that quail would nest so handy!

Harrier hawks often nest in the hay paddocks, so stock cannot interfere with their nests, hoping their young will be gone by the time the hay is cut. A pair of Hawks built a big nest in a large crop of oats one year and I used to drive my wife alongside the nest so she could observe the young chicks and all the left over scraps from the rabbits the parents had brought for them to eat. However, human contact was sadly their undoing. The chicks grew up to thinking that all humans were friends and they never ever flew away at our approach. One day, when one of the chicks was fully grown and was perched on a fence post on the roadside, a car pulled up. The bird never moved, the driver got out and shot it. I blame myself for the poor bird's untimely death. I caused it not to be wary of humans. My eldest son, Barry always kept a Labrador female dog for retrieving his ducks in the shooting season and always brought this dog to work. When we were pruning the orchard and stopped for morning tea, his dog would always sit by me, knowing that I would share a lot more of my sandwiches or scones with her than Barry would. But the dog also knew that Barry would have a special parcel of meat in his bag for her. That was a certainty as it meant so much more to her to share my food. Barry was sitting a little down the hill from me with his dog sitting behind him, right alongside me, with its eyes on my lunch tin. – watching and drooling over every bite I took knowing that before I got to the end of the sandwich, I would give it to her. When she finally saw my tin was empty, she placed her paw on Barry's shoulder as if to say, "Don't forget me as I'm right behind you," She always knew that Barry had something special for her in his lunch bag. Whenever we arrived back at the house, she would go straight up to my home and wait at the back door knowing that my wife would have brought some dog biscuits for her at the supermarket. My son always reckoned that there was no other breed of dog that had the appetite as great as a Labrador or the intelligence to know where to look for food. Strange how cats are so different from dogs. You can tell a dog what to do, but you cannot tell a cat.

We had a lovely black and white cat called Whiskers and one day when all my sons and I took off down the drive to go duck shooting across the road on the Mission farm, as we opened the gate, Barry said, "Oh, look, the cat is coming with us!" So I picked her up and carried her back across the road and said, "Go back home!" But to no avail. She wanted to accompany us all to the duck pond. When we got over the stile, the grass was long and wet making it difficult for the cat to make any headway. I had to carry it to the duck hide and it sat between Barry and me, purring its head off. I said to Barry, "What's going to happen to the cat when we all start shooting?" Barry just grinned. Next thing over came a flock of ducks, up went the four guns and as the birds dropped into the pond, the dogs splashed about retrieving them. I said to Barry, 'What happened to the cat?" He pointed to a post in front of the hide and there was Whiskers, sitting atop of the post watching all the dogs doing their job! The cat often came shooting with us after that, it must have enjoyed it. I would not mind betting it would be the only cat to ever go duck shooting! Cats just love company and some evenings when I would drive my largest tractor down the hill and across the road to rotary hoe a block of land to crop, the cat would sit in the middle of the yard to wait my return. When it saw the headlights of the tractor come across the road, it would run down the hill to meet me. On the way up the hill, I would change down into the lowest gear to rotary hoe a strip alongside a row of plum trees. As I passed each plum tree, going so slowly, the cat would climb up one tree and out on a branch, then scamper down and climb up another to keep level with me, all the way up the hill. It was just so excited! It was the only cat that ever rode on one of my tractors.

With large blocks of lettuce and cauliflowers, I always had endless trouble with rabbits. So often after dark, I would strap on my cartridge belt and along with my 12 gauge shot gun, drive one of my 4 wheel drive tractors with a good spot light, down the slopes where these crops grew, to shoot these pests that were devouring my crops. It so happened that Whiskers was extremely partial to rabbit meat, having dined on so many young rabbits it often caught. The moment Whisker's saw me mount that tractor with my gun, she would leap onto the bonnet, knowing a meal was forthcoming. The trouble was I had to be quick as the moment the spotlight picked up a rabbit; the cat was off the bonnet before I could even fire! Next thing the cat had the dead rabbit firmly held and was taking it back up the hill for an a la carte` meal.

My youngest daughter, Christine had two cats and when she placed two suitcases on her bed to pack for a visit to stay with me, one of the cats used to sit in one case, so that she could not pack it. They both used to get really upset when they knew she was going away. My daughter, whose husband was a deer farmer, had a young pet hind that followed her around the house everywhere she went. She had been bottle fed when the fawn had lost her mother. I am sure the animal thought Christine, was her mum. The little fawn was always putting her head in Christine's lap, wanting a pat. The fawn ate all Christine's roses, but she did not seem to mind – she loved the little animal so. It is amazing how all animals respond to food and care.

I soon found out the easiest way to shift a mob of cows with their calves was with a trailer of hay. One day I shifted all my cows and calves up to the top scrub block, but when I came up the next day to feed them again, there was a lost little calf walking and putting its head through the road fence looking for its mum. Apparently, the mother had the calf hidden in some rushes when I shifted them the day before. Fortunately, I had a young lad with me to whom I said, Kelvin, I want you to catch that little calf, but make sure you get it with your first try as once it knows you are after it, you will not get a second chance. The calf has four legs to run on and you have only two." Kelvin heeded my advice and made one mighty tackle, grabbing the little calf that bucked and struggled, then finally settled down as Kelvin hopped on the trailer load of hay for the journey up to the herd. Kelvin could not get over how the little animal settled down and was even snuggling into him by the time we got to the herd. The cows were all waiting at the gate as the noise of the tractor meant a load of hay was forthcoming. As soon as we entered the paddock, I said, "Now Kelvin, I'm going to look for the cow with a full udder and want you to put the calf down right in front of her nose and then walk away." The calf's mother took one sniff of the calf and pushed it away, spotted the open gate and took off like lightening down the hill to find her little one. What had happened was Kelvin, a heavy smoker, had smoked all the way up the hill while holding the calf, which became saturated with the tobacco smoke. This is what made the mother reject her offspring. Kelvin looked at me and said, "What do we do now?" I said, "Grab the calf. We will have to take it back down the hill to the mother, but don't smoke!" When we got down there the mother was searching the rushes for her little one. We placed the calf in front of her again, but she still rejected the calf as the smoke smell was still so strong. It took two days before the smoke wore off and they were together again. So take heed smokers – even cows know smoking is bad for you!

When one of my grand-daughters were quite young, she observed a family cat playing with a mouse and how terrified the poor mouse was as it trembled in agony knowing its last hour had come. The little girl felt so sorry for the mouse she rescued it, took it into her room and placed it in a large tea carton where she fed it. That mouse knew Gretchen had saved its life and was a friend, but it had to be a secret because she knew that mice were not allowed inside their house. One Sunday some visitors came calling and while all the family were entertaining them in the living room, the mouse got lonely and wondered where on earth its friend Gretchen had got to. It chewed its way through the carton and scampered up the passage to where it heard voices and ran across the living room in search of Gretchen.

One of the visitors called out, "I have just seen a mouse run across the room!" Gretchen's dad, knowing how his daughter felt about the helpless little creature, exclaimed, "Hello, hello, what is going on here?"

Poor little Gretchen knew she was in trouble, but to console her, they put the mouse in the poultry wheat bin which had a steel top lid, where the mouse would be safe from the cat and have all the food it could eat - in fact five star accommodation!

Gretchen who had only just stared school, used to check the bin when she came home each day to see if her little friend was all right and that wee mouse was always pleased to see her.

It is amazing how cats can tell the exact time! I had a young high school boy working for me, who once lived in the back country off the Taupo Road. Each day, with his brother and sister, he walked two miles to school, and their cat went too. But as the cat was not allowed in school, it used to get lonely and go back home. On the stroke of three o'clock, that cat was back at school waiting for the children to walk home with.

Even our duck shooting cat knew the time as each morning my wife would rise at 7.00am and her first task was always to put out a saucer of milk for the cat. On mornings that we packed lettuces for the market, my son and I used to start at 6.00am and of course Whiskers used to sit on the landing alongside us purring as we trimmed and packed the lettuces. But the moment the 7 o'clock time signal sounded on the shed radio, that cat was off like a shot up to the house for that saucer of milk. I reckoned it was the time signal that gave the cat the cue, but Barry; my son claimed it was when the cat heard the seven o'clock news. So we tried an experiment. We switched the radio off at 6.30am and when it came close to 7.00am we both started patting the cat and giving it food we had especially brought down for it. But 7.00am, that cat fought us off, ignored the food and high tailed it off up to the house for his milk. Hard to believe, but it is true.

Wild ducks always leave their feeding grounds before daylight breaks to fly back to the safe haven of the big lakes or sanctuaries from whence they came the evening before to feed. There are no duck more cunning than the mallard drake. They soon get wise to decoys, especially if it is a still day and they see no movement in the water. I never used decoys the second morning of duck shooting, but one second morning; I placed a pair of decoys in some rushes so it would be hard for the ducks to detect. A pair of mallards flew very high up out of range and the drake must have said to his mate, 'You keep up at this altitude and circle round, while I go down and check out these two objects in the rushes."

Down came the drake and hovered over the decoys with his neck stretched out peering at them and with one mighty, 'Squawk," Yelled to his wife, "outta here!"

I could have shot him almost sitting in mid air, but I let him go – I so admired his intuition.

One day when my daughter and her husband and a wild life ranger were returning from a walk up the local river, they startled a Canadian Goose that had just hatched out a clutch of goslings. The ranger noticed one egg left in the nest unhatched. He picked it up and handed it to Christine and said, 'Here, take it home and keep it warm and you will have a pet goose.'

"What on earth will I feed it on?" asked my daughter.

'Just what you feed all your poultry on," replied the ranger and so the little gosling grew up to be a famous pet. Gretchen used to take it to all the school pet parades and win first prize. They called the bird, "Gos" and when the family went on holiday, Gos would get lonely; he missed all the family so. However, Gos used to fly across the river to a neighbouring farmer who was building a new fence and spend the day with him for company, then fly back home when the farmer knocked of work for the day. This went on all the time the family were away. When they arrived home everything went berserk! The horse careed around the paddock, the ducks all quacked their loudest, the turkeys gobbled no end, the sheep dogs barked their heads off and old Gos squawked and flew around the farmyard in a frenzied excitement - all so relieved to see the whole family back.

Birds and animals have the same feelings as humans.

I have a very close friend, Bill Hoffman, who used to do all my buying and selling of my cattle for me. He used to buy 18 month old steers, which I would fatten and sell as three year olds. Every now and then we would have a steer with an ingrown horn that would penetrate its skull if left. So we had to bring a few of the steers into the yards and get the beast into the race to cut the horn back – a painful operation. After the job was done and we let all the steers out into the holding paddock to settle down, while we had a cup of tea, I noticed a couple of steers licking the head of the patient and consoling the animal who was lapping it up!

My chief helper, Wally Allen has a big, good looking German Wire Haired Pointer dog and when he reprimands it for some misdemeanour, it goes straight over to Wally's wife and puts its head in her lap for consolation!

I remember reading many years ago in an America Life magazine about the great comedian Bob Hope, who had a special van with compartments fitted to take all his children's pets to, would you believe, a psychiatrist who would have probably been laughing all the way to the bank! But Bob would not have minded - anything for peace on earth and goodwill to all pets – would have satisfied Bob.

A good friend of mine once gave me an Irish Water Spaniel, female dog in pup. Her name was Kitty and she bore 10 pups which was too many for her to feed, so I had to take some away. One of my sons took a female pup and called it Kitty after its mother, and another son took a dog pup and called it King. King and Kitty were different as chalk and cheese. King growled as a little pup while Kitty licked your hand even when you scolded her for being naughty. We always produced hundreds of tons of winter keeping pumpkins and when packing this product we had a lot of small hearth brushes to clean them with. One day I noticed King and Kitty, nose to nose, conversing with each other. I silently watched them to see what they were up to. King had apparently persuaded Kitty to go into the packing shed and procure one of these brushes. When she brought it out, King took hold of one end and together they took it over to the pumpkins store sheds and played 'take it off you' for hours. King was not game to go in and procure the brush, so he got the little lady dog to do it.

My youngest daughter, Christine, when a young child, used to always love to dress up in strange clothes to cause a laugh. One day, she found a pair of my old size 10 working boots and her granny's long discarded fur coat and one of her mother's oldest hats. So attired she opened the kitchen door where her mother was busy and said, "Hello Mother."

Her mother, who had a great sense of humour, burst out laughing and said," Go down and show the family." She clip clopped her way down in such heavy boots and Barry's curly retriever dog was the first to observer this unusually apparition approaching and went absolutely berserk, barking its head off. We all laughed and Christine took her hat off to reveal her face and head of little blonde curls, but the dog kept on barking furiously – it must have been the fur coat that upset it so.

All animals get used to a person's apparel which reminds me of a tragic incident that happened in England quite some years ago.

A farmer got dressed up in his best Sunday suit and donned his shiny new trilby felt hat, to go to church. As he drove past the barn he suddenly remembered he had not given his bull his daily ration of hay. He stopped the car and hurriedly entered the barn to feed the animal. The bull gored him to death. The bull would have thought the farmer was a perfect stranger in such clothes and would not realise it had just killed its best friend. Even if the farmer had spoken to the bull, the clothes would have been just too much for the animal to refrain from attacking the unfortunate victim. However, animals do respond to sound as I soon found out when feeding cattle. When I called them in winter, they knew it meant a bag of hay and my call in the summer meant a shift to a new paddock and much better pasture. When we first bought the farm, feed was short, so as we had large blocks of cabbage and cauliflowers, there was always a lot of rejects. We took up loads of these greens to the cattle. Even though many trucks plied the highway up to the area, our herd used to know the sound of our truck long before it came into view and they'd start bellowing their heads off. A few years ago, there was an article in one of our weekly magazines on how girls were doing much better than boys, in secondary education. They interviewed school principals and a psychiatrist to find out why this was so. Their only explanation was that boys were inclined more to sports and so girls naturally surpassed them. I was amazed to such learned people were not aware of the true reason, so I wrote my thoughts on the subject, to the editor. I explained that all female of any species of life on earth are more intelligent than males simply because of the sheer survival instinct of the species. If it was not for the shrewdness, the cunning and the cleverness of all the lionesses in a pride of lions, the male lions would starve. It is the matriarch in the elephant herd that leads them all to water in drought conditions and also finds ample food when the grass or foliage is scarce.

Even the female hyena is leader of the clan. I quoted in my letter as an example of female intuition, I had a paddock of winter keeping pumpkins growing in a huge valley, situated between two high ranges of hills, over 400 meters apart. A water course prevailed down one side of the valley, where several small dams intervened. One day, my eldest son, Barry, took a group of women down to hand hoe the crop. One of the ladies had brought her little dog with her. On one of the dams in the pumpkin paddock was a pair of mallard ducks with their brood of ducklings. The little dog from the city was overjoyed at the sight of the ducklings and thought what a great time it was going to have chasing them around the dam! However, mother duck had other ideas! She got out of the water and put on the 'broken wing 'act to entice the dog away from her brood. The dog thought this was even better. A fully mature crippled duck was too good to be true and so gave chase. The duck took that little dog 400 meters across the field, and then flew back to the dam to her ducklings. The little dog, frustrated beyond reason, finally made its way back and the whole process started again! What was father duck doing while this mum was away doing all the donkey work? Why patrolling the dam, nodding in approval of mother ducks efforts and telling the ducklings to dive when a Harrier Hawk appeared in mum's absence. That poor mother duck spent all day enticing that little dog away from that dam, but she saved her brood.

A typical example of female intelligence for the survival of the species. The editor did not print my letter, but he did write to me and said that he saw my point of view but explained that he couldn't print all the letters he received. Whether or not he thought I was being disloyal to my gender, I know not or whether he did not like to agree that the female of the species were more intelligent, I could not say.

Another incident a friend of mine had a lovely Labrador female dog which he fed well and took great care of. However, my friend often indulged in a well known male pastime in the evenings making his dogs evening meal times somewhat irregular. My friend had a wonderful mother who spoilt his dog no end with large amounts of food and great bowls of milk. Now, this dog was about to have pups but was concerned about his masters unusual feed times, so she had to give the matter a lot of thought. She finally decided that my friend's mother's wood shed would be the best place for her confinement. She bedded down there knowing that five star treatments would be forth coming. These pups had a double dose of female intelligence – a mother's intuition where to stay and my friend's mothers more than adequate food supply.

Not many people realize just how intelligence pigs are. The first thing a pig does when placed in a sty or pen is to circumnavigate the entire enclosure, looking for a hole to escape. If it cannot find one it has the capacity to make one. There has been more pigs escape their compound than any other animal. Having a huge tonnage of winter keeping pumpkins stored on the property, we had to keep pigs to consume the rejects. Our pigsty was situated at the end of a block of apricots and when we were pruning the pigs would hear the motor on the hydra ladders and would start calling out to us. When we answered them they would squeal all the louder until we went over and threw them some pumpkins. They would then grunt their thanks as we scratched their backs with a stick. Pigs make wonderful pets. There was a young lad named Andy Jones, who had a pet pig he used to take for a swim in the sea and his pig really enjoyed it. It was so unique, the local paper took a photo of Andy and all is mates surfing with the pig at the local beach.

I had a farmer friend who had a real back country farm on a remote area off the Taupo road. One day, when my friend, Alf Hindmarsh, that was his name, was driving his sheep on the road to his woolshed for shearing, a neighbour on his horse coming from the opposite direction called out, "look what's following your dogs", Alf looked around and there was a little wild pig that had lost its mother, tagging along with the sheep dogs. Being sheep dogs, they did not take the slightest notice of the little animal. Alf waited until all the sheep were yarded then easily caught the little fellow and placed it in a pen, giving it milk and food. It became a real pet and was eventually allowed to mingle with all the ducks, geese, turkeys, chickens and bantams, as a member of the farm family. They eventually called the pig, "Old Porker!" Farming in such a remote area with few deliveries of food supplies, Alf had a large vegetable garden well fenced off from the farmyard. To enter this garden, there was a swing gate with a huge spring that made it swing when pushed either way. Old Porker was quite intrigued by the way the family entered the garden by pushing the gate inwards, then emerging with loads of vegetables pushing the gate outwards. When nobody was looking, he figured a way he might be able to give it a try. When the time was right he pushed the gate open, ran over to a row of carrots. The moment he had pulled the vegetable, he started squealing at the top of his voice all the way to the gate and down to the farmyard where his friends wondered what all the commotion was about. Old Porker knew he was committing a felony, he knew he was not allowed in that garden, hence all the screaming as he knew he was doing wrong. Alf's whole family had come out to see what all the noise was about and found Old Porker's antics hilarious. It became a daily ritual for Porker to help himself to the odd turnip or carrot; and to the amusement of the whole family, he squealed at his wrongdoing, thinking he was going to be caught.

How pigs became wild in New Zealand was when Captain Cook exchanged pigs with the Maori tribes for fresh vegetables such as sweet potatoes, known as Kumara. Some pigs escaped and quickly multiplied and hence the name for wild pigs was often referred to as Captain Cookers. In fact wild pig meat became such a delicacy that the North Island of New Zealand was often called Pig Island in the early days and settlers from England often called the local people Pig Islanders. In turn, the New Zealanders called the new immigrants, "Pommes".

As an example of how intelligent Californian Quail are, we were leasing a small block of apricots off my neighbours, Norman and Mabel Lemmon; and it was their habit to have morning tea and then go out in their car shopping or visiting. The moment their car went down their drive, one mob of quail called out, "Cuckoo Coo; and another mob in a plantation answered in quail language. "Yes, we heard you!" They'd then go along with twenty to thirty quail from the hedge and an equivalent number from the trees, and zoom down on Norman's vegetable garden and tear the lettuce, silver beet, cauliflower and cabbage plants to shreds. Why quail are more destructive than other birds is because there are so many of them. I know the quail on my property which are over a hundred all told, are in the hedge waiting to see which way I take my tractor or truck, and then call out to each other their best plan of attack. I once planted a large block of cabbages for the market at the back of a section and being so busy with other work, never looked at the plants for 10days. When I did have time to see how they were doing, all that was left was thin, bare stalks! The quail had stripped every leaf! I abandoned the crop, but to my surprise, the plants recovered and produced an excellent crop of cabbage only a month later than normal.

Crows had always been the farmers greatest pest, when trying to grow crops, hence the 'scare-crow', a comical replica of a man standing stock still in the middle of the crop to scare the crows away. However, the crows are not silly, they just eat around it and the sparrows and starlings built their nests in it. When we planted expensive certified seed potatoes up at our farm, the crows pulled every seed up just to see what we had planted. They never ate one! They were just curious in case they were edible. I had to lie hidden in some tall bracken with two loaded automatic shotguns and some decoys made out of wireframes and black cloth and I shot 25 crows which was a record. I had propped up each bird I shot with wire which lured the crows over to me, but then, being crows, they had a count up and found 25 missing, so called off the exercise. They all flew away except one bird which perched on a tall poplar tree as a sentry to watch if I went home. The moment I would have left my post, they would have been back and my crop ruined.

However, in New Zealand we have a far worse destructive pest than crows – our native swamp hen called a Pukeko. A pretty bird, but a real destroyer of all crops. In many cases market gardeners have had to give up as Pukekos have put them out of business with their destruction. They too, pulled all our seed potatoes up and never ate them, but they ate all the water melons and when I planted carrots up at the farm, all that was left were long holes in the ground where the carrot had been. They eat young ducklings too, but worst of all, they breed all the year round. They lay 8 eggs at a time, so their numbers increase rapidly. If we shoot a hundred on our creek, two hundred would take their place, as nature does not stand a void.

When I grew green peas and lettuce, larks ad sparrows were the worst pests. The larks trimmed the rows of peas down like a hedge and sparrows devoured the pods when they were ready to pick. Keeping the pests off my crops was so time consuming, I found it hard to get the work done. I therefore worked out a plan, I went down to the local butchers shop and purchased a lot of large beef bones which still had fragments of meat left on them. I wired these bones on posts around the crops and the Harrier Hawks came and flew around the garden competing for the meat and scared the larks and sparrows away. A great saving in time and also cartridges! My youngest daughter, Christine used to call the hawks, "Daddy's policemen birds."

Even the grape growers despite the electric guns, have to use farm bikes and shotguns and constantly race up and down the rows of vines to scare away the birds, who are aware the electric bangers are only frighteners. The birds are not silly! A shotgun is the only real frightener for predators like the harrier hawk or falcon.

However, so much for pests. There is also a pleasant side to farming. One morning I arrived up at the farm just as dawn began to break, but the sun had not yet appeared.

There had been a slight fall of snow in the night about one or two inches deep and as I approached the paddock full of ewes with recent born lambs, I saw one of the prettiest sights I have ever seen. The sheep were still all sitting down where they had camped for the night and their lambs were all sitting up on the backs of their mothers to keep out of the snow. These ewes would have told their lambs to hop up there out of the snow. They benefitted not only from their mothers warm body heat, but the warmth of the full wool the sheep were carrying.

A new born lamb's coat of wool is very short and not much protection against snow or cold rain and that is why so many are lost in the winter blasts. It was just another example of female intelligence and real motherly care for the survival of the species.

One Sunday, when I took my wife for a drive up to the farm, as we passed the stockyards, I noticed a mallard duck take off by a gate and wondered what she was doing there. I was soon to find out! As I leaned over to release the latch, I looked down on the other side of the fence, where there was a shallow dry water course running down to the dam. Crouched on the flat grass was a clutch of ten, day old ducklings. The mother whom I had scared off must have left strict instructions to lie flat until she came back! I kept very still, not wanting to alarm them and beckoned my wife to come over quietly to view this pretty scene. We crept away ever so cautiously and on the way back, she saw the mother had returned and was taking them all up the hill to another pond that offered more shelter from predators.

What was so amazing, was the heed those little ducklings took of their mothers advice to stay so still. If only human children were so obedient, what an enormous amount of children's lives would be saved.

A classic example of just how vitally important it is for offspring of all species of life to be able to communicate to have parental guidance and instruction was demonstrated quite some years ago in an African Wild Life reserve. The authorities had decided that the elephant numbers should be increased, so they engaged some wild life operators to capture a number of young elephants where they were plentiful and transfer them to their new quarters.

I chose animals to relate this important function as they have rules just like we humans do, the only difference is animals do not break their rules where as we spend 24 hours every day, 365 days a year, breaking ours and then wonder why we have 800 people on death row in one penitentiary alone in San Quentin in California; and millions incarcerated in prisons around the world and yet still have the audacity to call animals dumb!

It was however, dumbness of the people who decided to choose immature young elephants to be transferred. When let loose, in a strange environment, without their parents, they were lost souls, orphans; they were like a ship without a rudder – no matriarch to guide them. They went on a rampage through the local village, frightening the inhabitants and damaging their dwellings and crops. The whole herd that had been transferred became disoriented delinquents. The head matriarch that leads the elephant herd is like the mother superior in a convent – her word is law! It is the matriarch that leads the herd to water in time of drought; and when foliage is short, to better grazing. Her knowledge and intuition is passed down to future matriarchs for the sole purpose of the survival of the species. Although the people involved in this tragic event had nothing but good intentions, they did not realize that the strong family ties and deep parental bonding played such a significantly important part in these majestic creatures up-bringing.

I had two friends living in a suburb and they resided at the far end of a cul-de-sac. They were in the habit of buying up stale loaves of bread from the supermarket and feeding it to the birds on their back lawn. A shallow creek ran through the village where many mallard ducks nested. The stream was over a hundred metres from the couple's home. I do not know how on earth that other duck found out about that food supply, I could only surmise it must have been flying low over the Cook's backyard and perceived all the birds dropping in at feed time and thought, "Goodness me – a free lunch – I must investigate this!"

It was not long before mother mallard was taking her brood of 10 ducklings around for a good feed. If there was no bread on the back lawn when she arrived, the duck would climb up the back steps and tap at the screen door and quack her loudest, demanding food. I was sitting having a cup of tea and this loud tapping began. I asked, "What on earth is that noise?" 'Its that duck wanting its breakfast. Go on Sonny, you'd better feed it as we won't get any peace until you do." replied Jocelyn. Now the Cooks had a huge ginger cat called George.

My friend, George the cat, being warned by mother Mallard, not to get any ideas, as she protected her young brood!

George and I were great mates, he would always come over to me for a pat when I arrived and when I dropped in with fruit, flowers and vegetables and the Cooks were not at home, George would come over to my car when I was opening the boot and tell me they were not at home, and then tell/meow his troubles to me saying how they had gone and left him all alone. The more I talked back to him, the louder he would meow. I used to send him a Christmas card with a twenty dollar note in it just for a laugh. Jocelyn used to send me one back from George, with a lot of meows, signed George. Jocelyn took a prize photo of the mother duck brood, gorging on bread and the mallard standing between her ducklings and George; reading the riot act and quacking at George, 'Don't get any ideas!" George was too well fed to bother with ducklings – I don't think he would have even chased a mouse.

When I was sixteen years of age, and old enough to carry a gun to hunt for game to put food on the table, as it was still depression days and meat was too expensive to buy, I had a friend who taught me how to hunt wild birds. His name was Frank Robson and he was known as the 'Dolphin Man" because he was always saving dolphins and whales. The authorities even flew him to Japan to try and influence the Japanese to stop killing so many dolphins. Apparently the Japanese staged dolphin extermination every so often as they ate their stocks of local fish. Frank had a hard job explaining to the Japanese, there was enough fish for everyone. Frank even wrote a wonderful book on saving the whales and dolphins; and was always called on when whales stranded. Frank finally became head trainer at the city's Marine land, his son Bruce also worked there too and Frank could not get over that when Brue had indulged in a few beers with his mates the night before, the next day, the dolphins would have nothing to do with him!

"What's wrong with them?" Bruce would ask.

"Nothing," Frank would reply, 'but they know there's something wrong with you!"

What amazingly intelligent creatures. Even though Frank was a hunter of all wild game, he was a naturalist and also a conservationist and had a wonderful relationship with all living things. He would talk to them and they would talk back, it was as if they understood every word he said, especially the dolphins.

One autumn we had a terrible gale; it blew in off the sea for three days. We had a 60 acre block of land all in vegetables fairly close to the coast and the gale blew in a dear little storm petrel into our garden. It must had been exhausted battling the wind as my son picked it up and brought it up to show me. I took it down to my old primary school and showed it to my granddaughter's class. The next problem was to get the bird back to its own habitat. I enlisted Frank's help who gave it to a fisherman with a trawler who took it out to sea. The little petrel had become so quiet and friendly, that when they let it go, well out to sea in the Pacific Ocean. It flew around and around and landed back on the boat. However, when the winches started up to haul in the net, the bird took fright and disappeared. When the haul was completed, the men went down to the cabin for a cup of tea and here was the little petrel, down on a bunk, quite happy away from the noise. I am not sure but I think it was 3 days before that little bird finally took off to roam the Pacific Ocean once more.

In conclusion, I would like to state that all the incidents, observations and experiences I have quoted would not have even scratched the surface as to what is taking place daily and nightly out there with nature. The geographical channel on TV with its fantastic photography and commentaries present a much better portrayal and we are a great source of education especially to young children. Finally from the tiniest ant to the largest elephant, their natural intelligence is boundless, so please do not say they are dumb! To think that man slaughters such majestic creatures for their ivory, for the manufacture of ornaments just to please the world's worst predators – mankind!

ALL ABOUT LIFE

Chapter 7

How we came about we will probably never know. Why we are here is quite obvious and can be explained in a few words. All life on this planet is born to survive. Survival is the name of the game. Whether it's bugs or bacteria; weeds or worms, fruit or vegetables, humans or animals, trees, flowers or flora, fish or birds, all forms of life on earth; their main purpose is the survival of the species. However, for this survival to actually take place, the oceans, continent and the Islands are the habitat of countless predators from insects to lions on the land and small fish to killer whales and whale sharks in the oceans. It is therefore a cruel and dangerous world out there, where so much life depends on their survival by the consumption of other living things. Mankind is no exception. Have you ever considered the number of cattle, sheep, goat, deer, pigs, rabbits, hares turkeys, ducks chickens, fish, lobster, prawns scallops, shrimp and other shellfish consumed daily by mankind? It is really the law of the jungle out there even though man has commercialized and modernised the procedures and attempted to control the survival of endangered species like whales, tigers, rhino, dolphins and others which is commendable. Although predators are provided with the cunning skills, claws, teeth that sever the jugular, the prey they eat was also equipped with big ears and amazing nostrils that can warn of an approaching predator. The extra large ears of rabbits and antelopes, the enormous leap of the impala deer, the radar of the pheasant and peacocks which warn the wild life of an approaching enemy. I once heard a commotion on my property in a large macrocapa tree by an implement shed. There was every kind of bird you can think of – blackbirds, thrushes, sparrows, chaffinches, goldfinches, fantails, starlings, mynahs, all kicking up an enormous row. On investigating, I found that all these birds had one of our native owls, known as a Morepork, bailed up in a tree. This owl hunts these birds at night and I have always noticed that when they fly, you cannot hear their wings – they are designed for stealth; so that birds cannot hear their approach. The owl seemed lost in the day light and its prey had discovered its day-time hide out and alerted all the other species – hence all the commotion. The owl just stood on its perch, unafraid of such a large intrusion. Despite their numbers this flock of much smaller birds seemed reluctant to attack their predator but they were letting the owl know who the boss in the daylight was! Despite all these predators that exist, the toll overall is small compared with the rate the prey are able to replace their numbers by their continuous urge and ability to bred. This immense, everlasting natural desire for all forms of life to mate ensures the offspring can carry on the survival of their species. Even the first purpose of the plants, fruits, vegetables, flowers, trees, shrubs – every kind of flora from ferns to the mighty Oaks, the tallest Redwoods and Douglas firs, all bear seeds that the species may survive.

As a grower of Brassicas in the horticultural industry, I must have raised millions of cauliflower, cabbage and lettuce plants over the 72 years I have operated. Occasionally, especially among the cauliflower plants, we would come across plants with no centre heart, which of course we had to discard. This meant with no heart the plant would not be able to produce seed. A pure malfunction of a genetic nature in the reproductive process. It may have been caused by lack of pollination, it is difficult to ascertain. All life is subjected to variances in the reproduction goals of nature. Even mankind is no exception. That male humans want to co-habitat with other males and females want to mate with their own gender, is nothing more than a genetic malfunction that can happen in any race on earth, but for reasons unknown, more so in some races than in others. The true causes have baffled Physiatrists, Doctors and Scientists for centuries, so like the reason for the heartless cauliflower plant, we may never know.

I once visited a South Pacific Island on behalf of my Vegetable Growers Federation, where there existed a small number of effeminate males and I observed how the elder mothers took extreme care of them. They even had a special name for them, which I can't remember, but it was some kind of ladies name even though they were really males.

The nearest the medical profession have researched this un-natural disorder has found that males who only prefer other males, had extra large pituitary glands almost the same size as females, which are twice the size of males. So although un-natural and abhorrent to the majority of people who have been favoured with normal genes of reproduction, for these unfortunate souls, it is not their fault! However, at the same time it is pathetic to see politicians from America, the United Kingdom and my country New Zealand, make political capital out of the plight of these unfortunate people by approving publically their support of same gender marriages. I myself could never refer to these lost souls as 'gay'. These people have made a vulgarity out of the word. A gay person is a happy, bright, delightful person – a little over frivolous perhaps, but certainly not a person afflicted with a genetic malfunction of their particular gender.

When one looks back in time to that famous film star, Rock Hudson and how his magnificent physical stature and handsome good looks, all turned to the tragic figure that finally emerged when he became afflicted with AIDs, tells its own story how wrong and disastrous this kind of living can be, yet it was not the film's stars fault – he was destined at birth to such a tragic end.

The enormous toll AIDs has taken on the African Continent also proves how important hygiene is in preventing such a devastating disease. Aids have to be handled similarly to cancer – prevention is far easier than cure. Cancer can be prevented by the correct diet; any nutritionist will tell you that! A various intake of natural, unrefined food such as healthy, correctly produced fruits and vegetables, whole grain products, like bran, oatmeal and wholemeal in natural form, not baked, roasted or burnt to a crisp so that it is well nigh indigestible.

Plenty of fresh fish, not smoked, is essential for a balanced diet too. The populations of western countries are the victims of commerce. The big food conglomerates, churn out millions of cartons and packages, of over- refined food, full of preservatives, all carcinogenic and people wonder why cancer can strike even young people today. It is why young people are dying younger and older people, who eat right, are living longer. The Russians banned red dye for years before many countries even thought about it. A little preserved meat may not be too harmful, but a steady diet is dangerous as the moment you prevent decomposition of fresh meat, other than freezing, and by artificial preservatives, you are inviting trouble. On my first ever trip overseas, I bought a fantastic book in Honolulu, written by a United States doctor who had sadly watched his father die of cancer of the colon. With all this doctors' vast knowledge and experience, he could do nothing to save his dad. However, it inspired him to study the causes of this devastating disease that takes so many thousands of lives in western nations, each year. His book was called; "The Save Your Life Diet" and it claimed that for two cents a day you could live a lot longer. That small sum was for two cents worth of Bran! The emphasis is the importance of whole grain products in our daily diet. I once read in another book, where scientists fed rats solely on white flour for 90 days and they all died. Weevil will not go into a bag of white flour, they seek the wholemeal, the bran the oatmeal and the pollard. We humans therefore are expected to eat what insect will not touch! A group of British doctors away back in the 1950's, visited tribes in Africa, to study their eating habits, to ascertain why they were never affected by heart disease. They found that there was so much natural fibre in their diet, their food intake digested in a few hours, where as people back in England, took up to four days. Asian populations do not have anywhere near the incidence of cancer and cardiovascular disease that western nations do. I can remember that well known golfer, Gary Player commenting, "When I see white flour and white sugar, I see poison!"

Young people in most western nations are victims of commerce who produced trendy, refined foods and drinks with so much artificial colouring, flavouring, and preservatives – all carcinogenic, along with unhealthy fast food; then wonder why their immune system fails. All wild life knows far better what to eat than mankind. Even our domestic animals we farm are not as healthy as those living naturally in the wild. All wild life grazes and browses on such a wide range of fodder. Wild deer for instance will browse on tussock, then have a chew at some flax, then at different species of grass and a nibble at some succulent trees foliage, that maybe vital to the unborn young of a pregnant hind. When I used to grow table grapes for the fresh market, hares often invaded my vineyard to consume the bark off the young wood in August when the mothers were carrying their young. Instinct guided them for the very purpose of their survival. Whereas people who farm deer shut them up in enclosures with mostly one variety of grass and consequently have to supply supplements such as Swedes and nuts. It is the variety that supplies the wide range of nutrients that keep the wild animals so healthy; whereas modern farmers are always dosing, injecting so much, you almost have to be a chemist to be a farmer of livestock today. I remember the first year I farmed 50 Hereford cows and I arrived up at my property early one morning and I observed one of the cows lying dead under the pine plantation. With the sad sight of her little calf snuggling up to her body. I was informed it is what is known as grass staggers – a lack of magnesium in the spring grass. Although I had fed them ample hay and mineral blocks, it was not enough. I was to lose four more that spring! Next year, I grazed the mob up in a rough scrub block, where they had a variety of bracken, fern, native grasses and tree foliage; and I never lost an animal!

That is why humanity has over 50 varieties of vegetables, many fruits, and cereal grains, all to be only slightly consumed to give the body a wide variety of essential nutrients to ward off disease and so keep the digestion and blood in top order. In the old days, we always knew that the old adage, "We are what we eat", was so true, here as today's youngsters believe mainly in, "They are what they tweet!" The whole world is not only in a financial crisis, but a digital dilemma as well. Online will soon be heading for 'Off line'. There is only one formula for good health and that is Fresh Air; plenty of sensible outdoor exercise and wholesome food. My daily work as a horticulturalist is extremely healthy when it comes to exercise. Pruning or thinning fruit tress you are constantly moving your arms and body, stretching and reaching. Although modern machinery has eliminated a lot of the hard work. I find hoeing the most advantageous form of exercise I perform. I also once read that the man with the hoe develops the cerebrum – if that is true, then as I have hoed since I was 5 years old, I am going to have to do a lot more if I am going to finish the book! Walking is also the best exercise a person can partake in; it is far healthier than running. Elderly people should never run or jog, as it puts too much strain on the heart. When people go to their doctor with heart problems, doctors generally prescribe three miles a day walk, preferably on the grass in their local park – not on concrete or macadam on roads. Obesity has hit the USA, England and even our own country, all through the wrong kind of diet and lack of exercise. I was once invited to present a paper, in New Zealand on large scale market gardening on behalf of my Grower's Federation to an Agricultural Science Conference at Massey University. I relished the opportunity to query the many attending scientists with why their overseas colleagues had destroyed the flavour, the succulence and worst of all, the nutrition in many of the new hybrid strains of modern varieties of vegetables.

"Look what you have done to the present day cabbage. It's a weed you could grow it at the South Pole." I exclaimed. "You dare not fertilize it or you would never pack it in a container! It is completely devoid of true cabbage flavour! The succulence and strong cabbage flavour of the old "Flower of Spring" type cabbage is lost forever"

Customers keep asking me, "Why do some carrots you buy taste like carrots and some do not?" Because some are hybrid where they have either destroyed the carotene in the carrot or weakened it. As an example, a new variety of seed was introduced some years back and as an experiment, a block was planted in a farm alongside the old popular variety known as Doon Major. When the crop was mature enough for consumption, they turned a large mob of sheep into the field, and guess what - the stock ate all the old variety before they even touched the new one. The new variety had more bulk, but no flavour and as I have already explained in a previous chapter, that nutrition and flavour are synonymous. - The sheep knew which was best! However, my son- in- law, who is a deer farmer and who is always giving me plenty of stick as regards to my hobby horse on nutrition, chose the new variety because of the bulk. This is the main trouble with genetic engineering; they have sacrificed flavour with no nutrition for excess yield. Years ago farmers in my country used to grow a Brassicas crop called Rape, which they used to fatten lambs on. However, the crop was so nutritious that pests such as aphid used to attack the crop, so along came the scientists with a new version of an aphid resistant strain. The very fact that the aphids turned their noses up at the new strain was because it was flavourless, which also did not appeal to the lambs either, as they did not fatten on it. Today the old variety is not available consequently Rape is no longer grown. A great loss to the industry all through the meddling with nature. I still grow old fashioned varieties of tomato, carrot, parsnip, pumpkins, cauliflower, potatoes, apples, apricots, plums, nectarines with flavour that would knock you down. Look what they have done to the strawberry – they have produced a beautiful bright, red berry, completely devoid of that ancient, true strawberry flavour. What use is the brilliant red berry if its magnificent colour conceals such poor eating quality? It is true that the old Madam Melba was an ugly shape and less attractive colour, but the flavour was what gave this most popular berry its name. Even little children have an instinct that can elude adults. My wife had a lovely, kind nurse that always treated her at the medical centre. Wanting to show her appreciation of the nurse's wonderful care, my wife asked me if I had any spare small cauliflowers she could give her. I grew a really old fashioned cauliflower called Snow Packer. It not only melted in your mouth when steamed, but it had the true flavour of a real cauliflower. Being one of the old types, it threw quite often, a few small heads which I always gave away, so my wife took Anne the lovely nurse, some. Now Anne, had two little girls and the youngest, a five year old, refused to eat the hybrid cauliflower her mother cooked for the family. She knew by the tastelessness they were of no consequence. However, when her mother gave her some Snow Packer, she asked for more! And the mother was very pleased. I gave my wife so many to take down to the nurse, this dear little girl painted a picture of me in my garden and gave it to my wife to give to me. The little girl would be in her twenties now, but I still have that painting. How little ones love to draw and paint! I once called in to a grower friend of mine at Pukekohe, on my way north to purchase some solid plaster columns for the veranda of our new homestead I was building on the farm. As we were talking, his little five years old brought out some paintings she had done to show me. My friend, Ian McDougal, explained to his daughter that I did not want to see them. The wee girl was crest fallen.

"But I do, I do, "I exclaimed. "What do you think I called in for?"

Kylee just beamed and gave me two to take home – I still have them.

A few years ago, I had the whole class of boys and girls from my old school, come up to my horticultural property to learn about gardening. They were so appreciative, they all sent me cards they had painted and drew pictures of me in my garden. A treasure I will always keep.

For many years I used to host students from Lincoln College in the South Island and Massey University in the North Island; who were taking a horticultural course. I always emphasised the importance of keeping the soil in good heart by continuously adding huge crops of oats or threshed ryegrass to build up the fibre. In the years of my winter lettuce production, I used to spread as many as three thousand bales of threshed ryegrass on the land which produced large heads of top quality lettuce in the middle of the coldest winter. The warm northern slopes and my provinces winter sunshine did the rest. I found out purely by accident the value of straw when added to the land. A neighbour once gave me a stack of hay that he no longer needed, as he was called up during the war. It was poor quality hay as it consisted of native grasses from the hill country. I had an old Chevy truck I used to cart the hay home in; and a cobber of mine, Ken Whittington helped me load it. Ken was up on top of the stack, tossing the hay down to me, when I dropped my fork. I jumped down to pick it up and exclaimed to Ken," There is a potato plant growing at the bottom of this stack!" 'See if there is anything on it, "Ken called out.

I pulled the haulm up and to my surprise, the growth was six feet long and at the end was a nest in the hay of 32 potatoes – all sizes of course, but quite a large number of big ones. That taught me the value of natural compost and fibre that needed to be added to the soil. From then on, I had a programme of spreading hay, growing huge crops of oats and regrassing and spelling the land. The scientists at the conference were amazed at the barometer I used for timing of the planting of early summer pumpkins. I did not plant until I saw the summer weeds starting to germinate- soil temperatures vary from Spring to Spring. There is no way you can beat the gun. When I saw the first signs of those summer weeds appearing, I put trays of pumpkin seeds in my wife's kitchen hot water cupboard. She tended them with loving care, keeping the seed moist each day and when the first shoots appeared, she would inform me they were ready and we would start planting. What amazed my old farmer friend, who helped us was the day our seed emerged above the ground, many self sown pumpkins plants from seed of the last of the crop, which were not harvested, appeared at the same time. Jack used to say to my boys," Your dad seems to know the exact time to plant – look at all those self sets emerging, the very day your dad 's plants come through."

One grower went shares with a Maori neighbour, Bob Haraki, who also had early land. In the late 1920's, Bob had been a Boy Scout and was one of only two boys to be picked from New Zealand to attend the world Jamboree in England. They could not have picked a better Ambassador to represent our country. Later in life, Bob became a Maori elder and spent most Mondays at the local courthouse rescuing young Maori lads who had got into trouble over the weekend. He called in one day to see me on the way home from the court and seemed quite disillusioned. He said," You know Jim, there's no such thing as delinquent children, there are only delinquent parents!" I had to agree with him, 'Yes, Bob, how true it is all about parenting!" Anyway, Bob's sharecrop partner informed him they would beat Jim by planting their pumpkins in July. Bob, being like all Maoris' (close to the soil and at one with the soil) exclaimed "Oh, I'm sure Jim would not plant that early." July was in the middle of winter, our coldest month. Bob knew the soil would not be warm enough. However, Bob's partner seemed bent on beating me to harvest the first pumpkins. All of August went by with no sign of any germination, then September – still no plants, while my seeds were warm, cosy and damp in my wife's hot water cupboard, waiting for the balloon to go up. On our warm, frost-free northern hillside slopes, we used to have plants raised in a glasshouse to crop early pumpkins in such warm areas, but still you could not beat the gun despite no frosts. You still had to take into consideration cold spring winds and cold southerly changes with snow on the ranges. All species of the cucbits family are prone to cold conditions so great care has to be taken. Sometimes in early September my eldest son, used to arrive at work and he was convinced that other growers on the flat had planted out their pumpkins while ours were still growing in the glasshouse. "Don't panic," I used to tell him, and always quoted Sir Francis Drake, "Time to win the game of bowls and beat the Spaniards too!"

I have seen big soft pumpkin plants set out in colder areas and actually diminish in size because it was just too early. The conditions were not suitable and when such plants get a check, they never fully recover. I relate all these observations and experiences solely to confirm how you have to work with nature never against her, for good results. When my good friend Bob Haraki passed away, it was the largest funeral I ever attended; an entire paddock on his farm was needed to hold all of the cars of the mourners. I lost count of the eulogies. Maoris' are known for their sense of humour and Bob was no exception. Bob kept a racehorse and one day took it to a two day meeting at a close Northern racecourse. On the morning of the first day, when all the trainers and owners were feeding their charges, Bob was seen beating up egg nog for his horse. All the others gave him plenty of stick for such a breakfast. However, Bob's horse won its race and the next morning at feed time, Bob got busy with his egg beater. There was dead silence but Bob smiled as he beat up the eggs and quietly asked, "Any comments?" An amazing man, with a wonderful wife and family, so sadly missed by so many. Truly a great citizen who set a wonderful example. There was quite an interesting end when I finished share cropping pumpkins with Bob. One day quite some time later, the General Manager of a Growers Cooperative market, rang me and claimed they had a new pumpkin supplier with a grade and pack equally as good as mine. "Oh, yes," I answered, "Who might that be?"

When he told me who it was, I said, "Well, I'm happy to take full credit for that packaging – he is my pupil!"

It was Bob's young son, Bevan, who had carried on growing. At the Market Division meetings for the Vegetable Growers Federation, I was always expounding the economics of grading and some of the younger members would often say, "Here's old Jim giving us a sermon on grading again!" But I often had growers thank me after following my advice. The Federation finally made me Chairman of a Grading Committee and it took me five years to obtain agreement to the specifications of over 40 vegetables with the retailers, wholesalers, Standards Association and growers. When it was finalized and presented to a select committee of the Government, they threw it out, saying it was ridiculous and would not work, yet some of the basic vegetable specifications were exactly the same as the Governments own grades imposed during the Second World War when the United States Joint Purchasing Board contracted NZ Growers to produce vegetables for their troops in the Pacific. After a World tour of the wholesale Horticultural markets, I found that there were mandatory grade standards for domestic supply in every country I visited and that my country was the only developed country in the world without compulsory grade standards for the domestic market. All because both left and right wing administrators did not want the cost of policing the regulation.

As a typical example, we now have some of the poorest quality produce being sold to consumers such as export Japanese Buttercup, squash rejects that are small, pale fleshed and too immature to be of any nutritional value. I have the proof as a buttercup grower. I am receiving twice the retail price; for wholesale orange coloured flesh, mature buttercups that the public are looking for and are prepared to pay for. Our daily papers are constantly being inundated with complaints of the poor eating quality of our local potatoes and the inadequate grading. A potato grower came to visit me one day and hopped onto the grading platform of our harvester and when he saw what we were discarding, he picked up a tuber with a flaw and said," I would get away with that in the market."

I replied, "You have just condemned your packaging by saying you would get away with it! When selling to the consumer, you should not be able to get away with anything; it is dishonest and not good business!"

One night at a potato growers meeting when I was expounding on the economics of grading, one grower spoke up, "No, we don't want compulsory grading, because when potatoes are short you can throw everything in." I replied that it was when potatoes were in short supply that you need mandatory grade standards more than ever as the price would be higher and the consumer had to be protected as well as satisfied or the grower would be out of business. I was once a member of a Government Constituted Potato Board and we spent two years working on specifications for the first quality grade standards for potatoes. Once again the Government, fearful of the cost of policing the standards, threw them out and as one inept member of the select committee claimed, "If the New Zealand public want to buy rubbish potatoes, then they should be allowed to."

The Board's request then to the committee was, "Would you support compulsory labelling if the consumer wants to buy rubbish, would you label it "Rubbish." This was also denied. The greater reward you receive for honest packaging and selling only top quality is not only the monetary return but your name and contact in the market place as it keeps you constantly with a finger on the pulse of the market which is essential if you want to stay in business. If you are still doubtful that honesty is not the best policy, this episode must surely convince you.

Two skiers were travelling up to a ski resort one weekend, when they ran into a blizzard and it got so bad, one of the skiers said, "We should not go any further as we will be snow bound and freeze to death. Let's go back to that farm house and see if they can put us up for the night." So they turned back, knocked at the farmhouse door and asked the pretty farmer's wife if they could be lodged for the night. She replied, "I'm afraid not, you see my husband has just passed away and it would not look good to have two strangers in my house. The neighbours across the road would be suspicious."

"Oh, well, "the young men replied," we understand, but would you mind if we sheltered in the barn then?"

"Not at all," replied the lady, "I will get you some blankets."

Next morning, the blizzard had blown itself out and the skiers returned the blankets, thanked the lady and went of their way. Ten months later, one of the men received a strange letter from the lady's lawyer. He was puzzled, so he rang his skier friend and asked, "You know that lady who let us sleep in her barn that cold night, you didn't happen to go to her house and pay her a visit during the night, did you?"

His mate replied," Well as a matter of fact I did. She seemed so sad and lonely and besides she was very pretty."

"And you did not happen to give her my name and address, did you?"

His mate went red, "Yes, I must apologize for asking that. Is there anything wrong?"

"Oh, no," replied is mate. "I have just received a letter from her lawyer, saying she has passed away and has left me the farm and all her money!"

So you see, business or pleasure it pays to always be honest!

ALL THOSE GENES

Chapter 8

It is a well known fact that it takes an enormous amount of genetic diversity to ensure the survival of all the species on our planet. Mankind or Homo Sapiens as we are known must be the most diverse form of all the species. Take the immense number of different races that exist for instance. Even with the world's population at 7 billion, despite a few look a likes, we really are all so different – colour, height, weight, temperament, disposition, eyes, nose, mouth, ears, complexion, teeth, intellect to name but a few. It is, however, this great diversity that enhances our survival. The age old argument of nature versus nurture is ridiculous as they are both complimentary and a part of one another. Nurture is a huge part of nature. Nurture can change the genes over time but the genes will always be the most important base that nurture has to work on. Take the U.S.A for instance, where people from all over the world have emigrated to and blended together as one nation and the world's largest economy, their prosperity and their wealth although now appearing to have reached its zenith, has produced over a few hundred years through this immense diversity of people, produced a race of its own. However, through their gigantic agricultural production, where they have fed the world at times, they have also overfed themselves and now have a problem with obesity among their people which proves how nurture over the years alters their genes. Another example is the islands of Japan with over 100 million people, had to fish the Pacific to survive, were notably a race of small people; but since the end of the Second World War have become Westernized both in industry and food consumption and have changed in stature. These two examples of the USA and Japan prove how nurture and nature are complimentary to each other and are really both part of a whole. However, it should be clearly understood that the genes are the most important because these are the base that nurture has to work on.

The most horrific example of how environment can affect the genes was of course proved in the Nazi's concentration camps during the Second World War, where millions of Jews were starved to death. The best genes in the world could not cope with such treatment of starvation and suffering, yet some did survive. This terrible example of cruelty to human beings imposed on other humans proves how closely tied one is nurture to nature, when the genes were denied nurture, they failed to survive. This shocking tragedy in German history also proves how human behaviour defies analysis.

There was once a wonderful lady named Vera Ballance who served in the Wellington District all her life as a Plunket Nurse. This lady was honoured by the Queen for her magnificent contribution to the care of so many babies during her career. When the contraception pill was introduced, she began to notice a difference in babies that were born after the mothers had been on this pill. This nurse noticed that babies born after their mothers had been taking the contraceptive pill for some years, had babies who seemed far less observant than usual. There was something unusual about their eyes she noticed. I believe the nurse informed doctors of this unusual change and made a study of the pill (which is a hormone) and found that traces were still in the blood stream, 11 months after it was stopped. Young children's behaviour problems have been debated over the last few decades and many causes like violence on television and movies have been blamed. It is a well known fact that alcohol and nicotine affects the unborn child. A hormone that interferes with the female menstrual cycle could be equally damaging to the unborn. Mankind is continually interfering with nurture and nature of humans, animals, fruits, vegetables, trees, etc. Back in the forties, scientists crossed a macrocarpa tree with a Lawsoniana tree. The Lawsoniana is a tall, graceful, upright tree with magnificent fern like foliage. The macrocarpa is a huge, spreading tree, used mainly for shelter. The result of this experiment was a conglomeration of the ugliest, weirdest species of all shapes and sizes of all the misshapen trees ever to be seen. They named the tree Arizonica; but it was at once discarded owing to its strange shapes, as there were not two trees that looked alike.

As a horticulturalist by trade, I have been astonished by the loss of old varieties of both fruit and vegetables which had the flavour and succulence that consumers cherished. Some of the modern varieties of fruit will not be touched by birds simply because there is no flavour. No flavour means no nutrition. Birds and animals will not touch crops that are non nutritious. Only humans eat non nutritious food! In desperation of losing these old varieties, I have planted a home orchard of plums, nectarines, apples and peaches that have flavour that would overwhelm you. When I give them to my friends, they cannot believe the flavour. Man has to stop playing 'God", and leave the genes to Mother Nature or it will all be lost.

There will be many post pill parents who will not agree with my observations, claiming they have well behaved, normal children, doing well at school and are everything parents could wish for. Good on them – how fortunate they are, but their cases only prove my theory on the importance of genetic diversity where there are no two people the same. In their instance the hormone had no affect at all. I once had a retired farmer who worked for me until he was 90 and he smoked all his life, but he had a policy of smoking one week and then having a week off. He never died of Lung cancer. I know he had an iron constitution – perhaps he had an iron pair of lungs too.

However, when a scientist invents a pill with a hormone that interferes with a female's body, it may only affect some and not others. Nevertheless, when a highly skilled professional person such as Vera Ballance notices such a dramatic change on observation perception of young babies, compared to pre-pill little ones, the whole question of contraception needs looking at. Never before in the history of civilisation, have there been so many youth suicides. Never before has there been so many autism and violent behaviours among youngsters. I read some 200 youngsters in the city of Christchurch in our country, have been suspended from school for violent behaviour like throwing chairs at the teachers. We all know that the wrong diet has a disastrous effect on people generally, but this effect of the hormone in the contraceptive pill, must also be one of the culprits. Look what Thalidomide did to the hands and feet of those unfortunate people. The more you interfere with nature, the greater our life is complicated.

I thought it was one of the many reasons why we got rid of that cruel dictator, Hitler, because he was altering the genes and trying to produce the master race; and here today, we are following those barbaric, despots' footsteps.

Commenting again on the violence on television and movies that is supposed to be causing the bad behaviour in today's youngsters. I cannot agree with this view as when we were young boys in the 1920's, we had plenty of violence in the movies during our early years. We had Tom Mix, Fred Thompson, and Hoot Gibson, Ken Maynard, tough cowboys playing cowboys and Indian. They were not very good at shooting – they fired hundreds of rounds and only hit a few Indians – some of them could not hit a haystack! Wyatt Earp, Buffalo Bill, Younger Brothers and Billy the Kid were much better shots. Then we had all the gangster movies with G Men with Tommy guns chasing gangsters through the streets of Chicago, sirens screaming, standing on the running boards of their cars, firing hundreds of rounds at their quarry, but missing most of them. Those were the days of real live gangsters like Bugsy Siegel, Pretty Boy Floyd, Bonnie and Clyde, John Dillinger, Al Capone, Dutch Schultz and all the mafia. As young boys we lapped it all up even though it was a bit of a joke. Occasionally there was a lovey dovey movie featuring Mary Pickford, Douglas Fairbanks, Billie Dove and Clara Bow, but they were too soppy for us boys – we loved the Cowboys and Indians and gangster films. In fact we all thought that America was all gangsters and cowboys fighting thousands of Indians. That famous writer Zane Grey wrote about them in novels like 'Riders of the Purple Sage' and The Lone Star Ranger" which were made in to films. War films like 'What Price Glory' and 'All Quiet on the Western Front' were classics in our time. Yet with all that violence we did not become violent, we did not go and shoot up classrooms of young children, like they are doing today. Bashing Policemen and abusing teachers never entered our heads. We had the utmost respect for authority. In all my nine years of primary school, I can only remember one burglary and one suicide - and we were horrified. There would only be one murder in the whole country, now there are homicides each week. I can only put it down to poor parenting, alcohol, drugs, substance abuse, poor diets and the use of dangerous hormones. I must say though, I have the upmost respect for the millions of young people around the world who have coped with this unusual sinister environment and am sure their achievements are mainly due to excellent parenting. I also feel a great sympathy for all the lost young souls who have fallen victims of the drug cartels, booze barons, fast food operators, refined food manufacturers and fizzy drink providers.

I was most fortunate to have parents with a great sense of values, who taught me how to avoid all the aforementioned, although there were no drugs about when I was young. Good parenting is the key to a child's future and survival. The recipe is a tremendous amount of love, mixed with the right amount of discipline to ensure a child's future. Even Dr Spock admitted he was wrong. Originally he maintained that if dear little Johnny started talking the roof off the house; he should not be stopped as it was a feeling of expression! I would make him put the roof back on and then help me paint it to teach him preservation! Then make him sleep a couple of hours in the rain that is if it was not too cold, to teach him the value of the roof over our head. I would probably weaken and make him a hot cup of Milo and bring him inside, but to all you silly sympathisers out there, if you ever read this epistle,(although I doubt you will) I would say I would be trying to save his future while you would be trying to destroy it. The quickest way to destroy a young child is to give it everything it wants. If you bring up children to believe the world is their oyster, you are destroying their ability to cope with harsh competitive, unnatural environment. As I am a product of the 1930's economic depression, this recent devastating disrespectful and lack of responsibility scenario has taught me that it is far easier to cope with adversity than it is to cope with prosperity. Adversity makes you struggle to survive and the whole process makes you strong. Prosperity and high living make you weak. In past centuries, kingdoms, dynasties and empires have all been destroyed by a surfeit of prosperity. Today the whole world has experienced over 65 years of continuous prosperity and now a serious downturn is about to engulf us, the spendthrift nations cannot take the austerity measures, so they riot and burn and protest; and I am afraid that worse is to come unless we instate responsibility and respect back into the masses. Instead of a privileged few, especially in the west (the East has not suffered this behavioural disease yet); the present civilisation is doomed and will finally destroy itself. There will be a clean slate and it will all start over again!

EARTHQUAKES

Chapter 9

I wish to acknowledge the book, Planet Earth, Earthquake by Bryce Walker and the editors of Times Life Books, for information used for this chapter, as indicated by *.

As a young 13 year old school boy residing in the small village of Taradale, situated in the province of Hawkes Bay, on the east coast of the North Island of New Zealand, I used to help out on a small mixed farm of orchard, cropping and dairying. Remuneration for my help never entered my head, as the sheer joy of having the privilege of helping with all the interesting farm work was payment enough, sometimes though a little remuneration was made.

At 5.00pm on January 31st 1931, I was sent to the far pastures to bring in a small herd of cows for their milking. As I drove the animals up the narrow race-way towards the cow yard, they became fidgety and nervous; and tried to back track to get out back to the fields from where I had brought them. The lady of the farm, who did most of the milking, saw my plight and came down to help me brandishing a big stick to coax the animals along. When we finally got the distressed cows into the yard, the lady looked at the sky and exclaimed,

"there is going to be a huge earthquake!"

I wondered what on earth she was talking about.

I was quite astonished at her prediction as I knew little about cow's behaviour and even less about earthquakes. I had experienced small quakes from time to time. But only when in my home, as small earthquakes are not usually felt outside or when one is moving about. I completely forgot about the incident and next day February 1st 1931, was a Sunday and my family and I accompanied some close friends, who owned a large touring car, drove us to a lovely sandy beach situated between huge limestone cliffs north of our town known as Waipatiki Beach. I had previously been fitted out in my new high school uniform, as I was to commence studies on February the 3rd in Form 3 at the Napier Boys High School. I was so proud of my new uniform, so of course, I had to wear it to the picnic. I was very careful to place my new clothes well up past the high tide mark to be sure of their safety while we were swimming in the surf.

The Waipatiki Beach sloped quite steeply down to the sea and in the afternoon about 2.00pm, a strange thing happened. The whole bay became disturbed and was covered with meter high white water rollers. These waves came sweeping into shore with massive force, although it was a perfectly still, hot summer's day and without a breath of wind. Little did we realize that the sea had risen right up past the high water mark and it was nowhere near high tide. The next thing we knew was all my new high school uniform was floating in the waves! Luckily there were three strong swimmers in the party who rescued my clothes, one by one. Unfortunately, I had to journey home wrapped up in wet towels as my clothes were naturally saturated. Travelling home along the coast road, which was high up above the beach front, we observed shingle, seaweed and other debris washed up all over the road and even down into some of the coastal lagoons across the highway. Being so young and ignorant of the works of nature, it never entered my head that there was a connection with the rising sea and the lady who had predicted the earthquake – as I had completely forgotten about her outburst. The next day the seas had not abated, but on Tuesday, the seas had quietened down and everything was so still. Then at 10.45am, the whole province was hit with a 7.9 earthquake that devastated the towns of Napier and Hastings, killing 258 people and raising the land over 2 meters. This emptied an inland seawater lagoon of 7000 acres and stranded thousands of fish and stingrays.

It was the first day for children to be back at school after the summer holidays, and to be the day, I was to start high school. But as I had had to travel home from the picnic wrapped in wet towels after nearly losing my clothes, I had caught a chill and was confined to bed. I had a very high temperature and my mother had come to my bedside to sponge my face with cold water, however the quake struck at that moment and the water went all over me. I was thrown out of bed, my mother and I crawled to the passage, as it was impossible to stand up to get to the front door.

By this time the quake had developed into massive vibrations which were so violent it is impossible to describe. I kept saying to my mother as we clung helplessly together,

"What is it, what is it?"

She replied, "It's the end of the world."

We had no idea it was an earthquake because of the intensity of the vibrations. It lasted about 2 ½ minutes which is a long time even for a big quake; and it was not until it was over and we could stand up and run outside onto the road, where we saw the electric power poles still trembling, that we realized it was a huge earthquake. We were all too frightened to go back inside our homes as the aftershocks scared us so. It so happened, that the house we lived in, and in which my mother and I had endured the quake, was built by my father. It was Ferro concrete with 4 "wide walls built on a concrete, floating foundation - that is a wide, deep foundation under every petitioned wall, of every room; consisting of 3/8" steel rod, both perpendicular and horizontal reinforcing and the strongest concrete mix of four of shingle to one of cement. The house never even cracked with the earthquake and even the chimney withstood the quake. Whereas everyone else's chimneys collapsed because they were built of brick and ours was made of Ferro concrete and built into the house. The house remains to this day, as solid as the day it was built 83 years ago, which proves that earthquakes do not kill many people. It is mostly man's construction; and tsunamis that cause the death toll to be as high. The Napier Township built mostly of bricks and mortar and on reclaimed land, did not stand a chance. Likewise the building (CTV) that collapsed in the recent Christchurch earthquake that took the lives of 113 people in one building, is a classic example of poor construction. On the night of the February the 3rd 1931, we were all too frightened to go back into our homes to sleep as the noise of the aftershocks was so disturbing. We slept under a willow tree in the neighbour's yard under a big tarpaulin, while some slept on mattresses; others of us children slept on the ground but with a pillow and that was when I found out what earthquakes were all about.

A monument to stability, the Ferro Concrete Public trust building that withstood the 1931 Napier earthquake; while all around collapsed.

The moment I laid my head on the pillow, I heard an explosion deep down in the earth, "Boom!" it went, then a couple of seconds later, just another slight quake. These explosions went on all night, five or six minutes apart making it almost impossible to sleep. It was then that I realised that earthquakes were the result of deep underground explosions, but at that stage I was at a loss to know what caused the explosions. Only after travelling around the world, visiting and studying volcanoes, especially on the big island of Hawaii where Maunoa Lou, Moana Kea and Kilauea (the latter being one of the most active volcanoes in the world) are situated.

When visiting the volcano house we were informed by our guide, that the people always knew when an eruption was pending as the whole area around the volcano began swelling and rising, in fact she told us, that the very building we were sitting in, the ground under it was rising. And sure enough, not long after we arrived home Kilauea erupted. I am certain that this was exactly what happened when that small herd of dairy cows refused to go into that cow bail, they were picking up the movement of the magma as it resonated below the earth's surface as it built up to the ultimate explosion on February 3rd. Likewise, the rising sea water was caused by the same process. The birds, animals and even fish have extraordinary perception of underground movements of rising or exploding magma. Male pheasants, on my property, give out distress calls at the slightest explosion. When my son and I were working in our market hillside garden, the pheasants all over the property gave their distress calls one afternoon and the next few days the same. I remarked that there must be something cooking underfoot and upon arriving home after work, I asked my wife, if there had been a quake. She replied, "No, but I heard the pheasants call."

The following week there was a slight quake and the week after that, a 6.5 quake in Gisborne, a town almost 120 miles distant as the crow flies. Those pheasants were picking up the initial movement and preliminary explosions prior to the main quake.

In another instance, a close friend of mine who worked on a property in Central Hawkes Bay, informed me that prior to a medium sized quake in the area, the farm horses careered around their paddock in fright, well before the ground shook.

Another incident happened in Australia. An ancient continent where earthquakes are a rarity, a lady who trained race horses in Newcastle in New South Wales, could do absolutely nothing with her animals prior to quite a severe earthquake that struck the area in the early 1990's. Although the death toll was light, there was however, considerable damage. The residents were startled at such a rare event and became even more concerned when a local lady claimed she could predict the next earthquake and named the time of 5.00pm on a certain date. Some of the locals, alarmed at the thought of another tremor, began ringing up the lady horse trainer to enquire how her horses were acting, on the predicted day. The lady replied, "They are eating out of my hand!" Of course, there was no quake.

One thing I have observed over my life time, is that the more ancient the country or continent is, the fewer the earthquakes; probably something to do with the dying downstages of the planet's cooling process. Whereas my country, New Zealand, although close to Australia, is an extremely young country, which is commonly known as the' shaky isles", experiences a large number of quakes annually from the bottom of the South Island to a line in the North Island about 70 kilometres past Lake Taupo, the old crater, which according to geologists was one of the world's largest eruptions when it disgorged 100 cubic kilometres of rocks, pumice and ash over a large area of the North Island. The area is also where our three active volcanoes are situated. About 150 kilometres past this line to the North, is our largest city, Auckland, where there are 49 extinct volcanic cones of no great height and where earthquakes never occur unless an extremely deep seated earthquake on a substantial magnitude in the southern part of the country and that is felt over a huge area, then the Auckland district being so far from the epicentre would receive only slight movements.

Over my lifetime's experience of local earthquakes, I have found that if the quake is a slow, swaying motion, that kind of movement means you are a long way from the epicentre and that it is always heavier a great distance away. Whereas if the quake is a sudden jolt, severe or slight, it indicates you are close to the epicentre.

One Sunday afternoon, when my four sons and I assembled in our large yard by our pack house with our retriever dogs, preparing to spend the evening duck shooting, there was a loud rumble and as I looked down our curved driveway, the ground was folding like paper in about foot high waves coming towards where we were standing. The epicentre of that earthquake was about 55 miles south of us. A duck shooting friend of mine, Colin Wood, was travelling along the Takapau Plains in his car, when the road started folding in metre high waves, he claimed he would never have believed it if he had not witnessed it. The Takapau Plains were only a few miles from the epicentre. My friend too, exclaimed the folding of the whole landscape, including the road were like paper.

A couple of days after the 1931 earthquake, I was still laid up in bed from the fever. The lady, who I had helped with the milking, kindly called with some goodies for me. She was quick to remind me,

"Did I no tell ye there was going to be a big earthquake?" she exclaimed in her broad Scottish accent. I had to agree she knew what she was talking about, even though I was too young to realize just what the cows were picking up. But she knew!

After experiencing the devastating earthquake of 7.9 magnitudes in Hawkes Bay, in 1931, I made my mind up that I would study seismology and volcanologist throughout my life time to try and ascertain exactly what causes such frightening upheavals. Consequently, I have spent 81 years in the study of earthquakes and volcanic eruptions, both of which I am certain are related; even though the new breed of scientists think otherwise.

In 1906, San Francisco experienced an 8.3 earthquake that along with the fire destroyed the city. It so happened that local geologists, after studying and experiencing so many after- shocks, came to the conclusion that earthquakes are caused by underground explosions, but could not explain what caused them. They came really close to solving the true cause of earthquakes.

Because earthquakes are spawned so far below the earth's surface, probably from the planet's molten interior, prediction is well nigh impossible. Mankind will never be able to probe the earth's 'plumbing' system by which variable quantities of gas enriched magma are propelled upwards towards the lithosphere where pressure is maximized until it explodes; thus shaking and rupturing the surface of the earth - known as earthquakes. Although birds and animals are able to pick up the movement of magma well before the final explosion by their extraordinary radar perception, even if they could communicate to us, they could never indicate where or the precise time, how severe or how slight the tremor maybe.

The mechanics of seismic activity has always been and still is, most complex. * With the Alaskan earthquake of 8.3, on Good Friday 1964, over 100 square miles of the earth's surface was heaved upwards or dropped downwards. For a 100 miles inland, north and west of the fault plane, the land had dropped 2.5 and 7.5 feet. For a 100 miles south and east of the West Coast Islands, the sea floor had lifted an average of 6 feet, with a measured maximum on Montague Island of 38feet; while along a line parallel to the fault from Hinchinbrook Island, southwest to the Trinity Islands, a wide area of sea floor had been raised up to 50 feet and had thrust up the massive amount of water that had caused the great Pacific tsunami. The intrusion of water into the air above it, in turn, caused the atmospheric disturbances powerful enough to ripple the atmosphere 50 miles above the earth.

All the afore mentioned geological changes that took place in Alaska through the gigantic forces of nature, while important to note and record, are only the result of such a catastrophe.*

The dramatic changes that took place, explain nothing of the cause of such a force that made a complete transformation of the landscape and seabed. Yet it was however, the Alaskan earthquake that goaded young scientists with profound geological aspirations to solve once and for all, the exact forces which cause such upheavals. For the next 15 years, these young geologists thinking they were onto something worthwhile; and with profound geological interests to solve once and for all the causes of the forces, which are responsible for such earthquakes. For the next 15 years these young scientists began to transform the earth's sciences by putting old theories, which explained so little, to rest; and by challenging their elders with their new hypotheses.

Because of the hitherto previous ignorance of what made the earth's surface rupture and shake, these young scientists found a ready market for their hypothetical theories – a responsive ear and because there had never been a sound logical explanation of the exact cause of earthquakes, a puzzled and receptive public, along with the academic fraternity, were only too eager to accept their theories, despite the fact that they could not be proved. The earths" surface is made up of a disputed number of tectonic plates, floating on a sea of magma, is nothing but a geological impossibility, in my view.

In the first instance, scientists are not all in agreement as to the number of plates, some say 6, others 8, and some 12. For many years there was no "Hawaiian Plate"; and when queried about the volcanic and seismic activity thereabouts, especially on the big island, it was explained that the area was an exceptional "maverick". I venture to claim the whole surface of the planet is a "maverick". Eruptions and seismic activity can happen with little or no warning, anywhere on earth. However, it was not long before the scientists conveniently invented a "Hawaiian Plate". These new scientists fail to realize that earthquakes can occur anywhere, at anytime – there is simply no rule or pattern.

*On February 8th 1750, Londoners, in England, were startled by an earthquake. It was not that strong but the sudden jolt rattled windows, shook furniture and sent people hurrying onto the streets. It was particularly disturbing as London had only experienced one tremor in the last two hundred years. A month after the February quake, a second and more powerful quake hit London. This tremor knocked down chimneys, rang numerous church bells, toppled buildings and threw the whole city into a panic. During the next few months, three more tremors hit the British Isles, causing no great damage, but a great deal of concern. Consequently, following these disturbances, there was immense speculation and miscalculation as to the causes of earthquakes.

About 50 papers were presented, but did little to throw any light on the subject. The intense concern raised by the London quakes was overshadowed five years later by a cataclysm that reduced the city of Lisbon in Portugal to rubble.* Such events, so unusual in Europe, only verify how "maverick", the planet can be. The recent quakes in Christchurch, New Zealand, confused the local geologists because they did not occur on the Alpine fault line. Earthquakes do not have to happen on a fault line. They are the result of earthquakes, not a cause of. The reason they often happen on a fault line is because it is a weak spot in the earth's crust, where extreme quantities of gas enriched magma congregate, to explode. Californian geologists became quite upset and confused when a large quake struck Northridge in that State, in 1994, because it didn't happen on a fault line. They solved that problem by inventing an underground fault line which they had not known previously to have existed. Incidentally, the Northridge quake produced 12,000 aftershocks – that's a lot of explosions! In 1811 and 1812, large tremors in the American state of Missouri changed the course of the Mississippi River. How do the new scientists account for such tremors that happen so far away from the edges of these so called, "grinding, slip sliding Tectonic plates?" *One of the first moves these new scientists made was to adopt the theories of a German meteorologist, by the name of Alfred Wegener, who trained in astronomy and geophysics. Wegener had a theory of Continental Drift, which he surmised that at one time, the continents were all just one large land mass and later broke up to drift apart to where they are today. Wegener's amazing hypothesis was greeted with hoots of derision from the scientific community. One colleague claimed that Wegener's methodology consisted of an initial idea, a selective search through the literature for corroborative evidence, ignoring most of the facts that are opposed to the idea. Despite that fact, Wegener's evidence was extremely thin and not much of a springboard from which to jump to such dramatic conclusions.* In the years ahead, geologists began to adopt Wegener's prophetic vision –perhaps, I would suggest, because there appeared to be no other course.

If the new science of earth mechanics suggests, that these hypothetical plates are sliding, slipping and grinding against each other, causing massive earthquakes, the geologist still cannot account for the colossal energy and force which propels immense areas of land mass and seabed to be thrusted upwards. Their theory also does not explain the thousand of minor earthquakes that occur around the globe each year.

According to some scientists, there are 1400 quakes each day around the entire earth. Furthermore, all quakes, large or small, have an epicentre, which can only imply an explosion and when we have such stark obvious evidence in the violence and force of volcanic eruptions, where immense amounts of magma emerge after pre-eruption earthquakes, have exploded and broken through the previous eruptions cooled and hardened seals, the process proves that the only difference between a volcanic eruption and a deep seated earthquake, is, one is surface explosion and the other a sub-terrainian one; but both of the same explosive material. To justify their hypothetical plate theory, the new scientists overcame this problem by insisting that there are two kinds of earthquakes – tectonic and volcanic. I venture to claim that Mother Nature is not that complicated, it is mankind that complicates all the simple answers involving the earth's mechanics. I also claim however, that my explanation of the true cause of earthquakes will never be accepted by the new scientists, because they would lose all their funding which is colossal and on- going, simply because their hypotheses can never be proved, whereas my explanation is based on first-hand experience and hard facts.

Furthermore, the Tectonic Plate theorists claim that New Zealand lies on the edge of the Pacific Plate, which is sliding under the Australian Plate; yet at the same time, these geologists claim that this same Pacific Plate is sliding under the North American Plate! How can this huge plate move in two different directions at once without parting somewhere in the middle?

Also, if the plates are moving, what is replacing where they have come from, as the earth is still covered in crust? Likewise, these plates if they were really factual, would not only have just started moving since these new generation of scientists supposedly discovered them, they would have been on the move for at least three billion years, so according to their calculations, New Zealand should be at least halfway to India by now! Instead, New Zealand is still rising and not moving anywhere. In my short lifetime, I have witnessed an over 2 metre land rise, which gave the city of Napier (that was previously surrounded by an inland sea of 7000 acres and many tidal estuaries) new dry land which now has thousands of residential homes on it and a large farm that produces the best stock in the dominion, because of the soils rich mineral content, having been once under the sea.

In a paper presented by Lynn Sykes and two Lamont colleagues, Jack Oliver and Bryan Isaacs, recounted a global future of moving plates and demonstrated that the accumulating seismological data supported it. The entire surface of the planet, they wrote, was divided into half a dozen or so immense plates. Half a dozen or so?

The "or so", could mean any number, making the hypothetical Tectonic Plates theory geological nonsense. Their similes and metaphors that describe the movements of these jostling, slip, sliding plates are ludicrous to say the least. Their theories are not based on fact, therefore are not scientific.

These new scientists know full well, we are never going to be able to probe the massive depths below the lithosphere to prove the existence of these plates, consequently, they can continue to exploit their hypothetical theories to a gullible public who are unable to refute their findings. The new scientists have great difficulty in explaining the seismic activity great distances from the edges of these hypothetical plates or where they are supposed to collide producing earthquakes.

* Some of the strongest tremors ever experienced in North American had occurred in 1811 and 1812, in Missouri and Arkansas, virtually in the middle of the North American Plate. On December 16th, 1811, at 2.00am, the first quake struck at New Madrid. Great tracts of forest came crashing to the ground, huge fissures opened up and the terrified residents reported flashes of lightning and the air heavy with

sulphurous vapours. Two more quakes struck this Midwestern frontier in the next few months with great severity; The second of these was so violent it rattled windows and agitated chandeliers in Washington D.C., stopped clock pendulums in South Carolina, set church bells tolling in Richmond, Virginia and awakened residents in Pittsburgh, Pennsylvania. In nearby Kentucky, it was reported that the ground rose and fell inwards. By the time the earth stopped shaking, the landscape had changed beyond recognition. Thousands of acres of prairie had been turned into swamp; a lake bed had been raised to become dry land. New Madrid, which was situated at the epicentre of two of the quakes, had been levelled and the land slumped 15 feet. Islands had disappeared from the Mississippi river and in places the banks had collapsed, temporally damming the rivers flow. Efforts to explain these quakes continue until today.* The Tectonic theory cannot be applied in this area so far from the edges of these hypothetical plates.

If the new scientists could even prove that these plates existed, because of my experiences and observations, I would still doubt them being the cause of triggering earthquakes; as in my evidence, along with nature's history and so obvious geological strata and terrain evidence, would prove otherwise.

Some years back, there was a series of 3.5 to 4.5 fairly deep-seated earthquakes in the lower north island of New Zealand. Some fairly close to the capital city, Wellington. In 1855, Wellington experienced a huge quake that raised 75 miles of coastline, 15 feet. The local geologists, always keen to predict the "Big One', started speculation about what these small quakes meant. I wrote to the paper saying that so many small quakes could mean that the pressure was being released gradually, which was much more acceptable than a 'Big One". Of course I could have been wrong, but as it happened, the quakes died down and Wellington was saved.

A lady from the capital persuaded me to contribute to a video she was making of the Napier 1931 earthquake in which I gave an account of my experiences. The video has been shown in the Napier Museum. The same lady once informed me that her young daughter was almost too frightened to go to sleep at night because geologists were suggesting that Wellington was due for the "Big One". I assured her that it may never happen in her lifetime and how wrong it was to frighten people, especially children. Of course, it could happen tomorrow or in 200 years time, but not necessarily under the city. It could be well out to sea, on top of the South Island, where deep seated quakes sometimes occur. I happened to be in the top storey of the St George Hotel in Wellington, the night of the Inungahua earthquake, at the top of the South Island, which is across the Cook Strait from Wellington. I was attending a vegetable Growers meeting in the capital and a Chinese delegate from the Auckland area, where they do not experience earthquakes, came rushing onto my bedroom, querying,

"What to do! What to do?"

I told him, as it was a swaying motion, it was a big one, far away; and to go back to bed and put his head under the pillow.

Later we learned that it was quite a big one. Eight storeys up, I told him I would not recommend the lift or even the stairs. Recently, I was asked to give an account of my experiences of the 1931 Napier Earthquake, to a large primary school, in Napier, where one of my great grandchildren attends. Because I, along with my mother had endured such a frightening experience, I did not want to scare such a large group of youngster, so I began by telling them that earthquakes were as natural as a thunderstorm, only a bit more devastating and if it was not for earthquakes, our country would not have existed. I really should not have worried, as the children were so interested that when question time came, about over 30 hands shot up; some of the queries were hilarious. One little girl wanted to know the colour of my new school uniform, that had been washed out to sea, when the waves came up. Another asked if anyone was able to save any of the fish that were stranded when the inland sea was drained by the large uplift of the coastline. They asked so many questions that the teacher called a halt, thinking I might be getting tired! But I quite enjoyed their queries and besides, I did not want to let my little great grand-daughter down!

As one of the few remaining opponents of the new scientist's theory of entirely different causes of seismic events and earth mechanics, I did not mention the Tectonic Plates or Continental Drift, to an audience so young – leaving it to their better judgement as they matured. However, I will never, ever understand this new scientist's theory of two kinds of earthquakes; Tectonic and Volcanic, when in my view, volcanic eruptions and earthquakes are of the same material.

Take the Tarawera Eruption on June 10th 1886. The ground began to shake in the centre of the North Island, in the Taupo area, around midnight. The quakes continued for an hour, then just after 2.00am, there was a fierce earthquake followed by a tremendous roar. Then the first of Mt Tarawera's three craters blew up and fire and lava belched out to a height of 1000 feet. By 3.30am, a great rift 9 miles long had opened up. Fireballs, lava, and mud bombarded the area until 6.00am. The eruption scattered mud and ash over nine thousand square miles of the Bay of Plenty district, burying two Maori villages and killing 153 people. Casualties were light because the region was sparsely populated. Surely this proves that earthquakes and volcanic eruptions are so closely related. I believe it is constantly being proved that earthquakes can occur anytime, anywhere, without any volcanic activity, but you cannot have a volcanic eruption without pre-emptive seismic disturbances.

On September the 29th 1955, the Kamchatka Peninsula which juts downwards from the Siberian landmass to within a few miles of the Kurile Island was jolted by an earthquake - quite a moderate one. During the next week, there was a minor earthquake everyday and by the end of the third week, more than a 100 tremors were rocking the peninsular every day, which is typical of a gradual build up of gas enriched magma prior to a volcanic eruption. The epicentre of these quakes happened to be in the vicinity of the Bezymainny volcano which had been quiescent for so long it was thought to be extinct. On October the 22nd, the quakes had increased to 200 a day and their number increased to 1300 all told. On that day the mountain began to erupt. As the mountain spewed out ash steam and ashes, the number of earthquakes increased to 450 a day. For a month, a plume of ash, five miles high, spread out from the volcano, reaching the Pacific Ocean, 75miles away. By the end of November there was a sudden drop in seismic activity and a simultaneous decline in the number of eruptions. For four months the volcano and the earth were quiet. Then on March 30th 1956, Bezymainny literally blew its top off in a stupendous eruption of molten lava, not just ash and steam. The blast pulverised the top of the mountain, created a mile wide crater and blew down trees 15 miles away. Simultaneously, a large earthquake rocked the Kamchatka Peninsula. After the main blast and accompanying tremors, both seismic activity and eruptions weakened dramatically. By June, the mountain and the earth were again still. During that 8 month period, there had been more than 33,000 earthquakes.

If this enormous seismic and volcanic event does not prove the source and cause of earthquakes; and the gigantic power of explosive gas enriched magma to constantly shake and finally erupt with the force to provide such concrete evidence as to the obvious and true cause of earthquakes, then nothing ever will!

I wonder how Plate Tectonics would account for the following.

In a small fishing village in the Bay of Naples, named Pozzuoli, some years back, and the whole village began to tremble and shake. The quakes were not heavy, just constant, but quite nerve –racking. The shaking kept going day and night for so long, the inhabitants could put up with them no longer. They abandoned the village! The fishermen returned each day to man their boats for their daily tasks, and then left the deserted town each evening, when they returned from the sea. How would the new scientists account for this unusual seismic disturbance, with no plates handy – would they be Tectonic or volcanic shakes? My explanation is the Bay of Naples is an old caldron, rich in the past volcanic history; a small amount of magma has been activated and is thus causing such constant seismic explosions.

I have never heard whether these constant small tremors ever ceased in this small Italian fishing village, however I'm pretty certain they would have eventually died down. I am only searching for the truth, a rare commodity in these unusual chaotic times, but I have no hesitation in concluding that the seismic and volcanic event that happened on the Kamchatka Peninsula clearly demonstrates like many other similar events, the origin and true causes of earthquakes and volcanic eruptions when extreme quantities of gas enriched magma, moves under the lithosphere, to explode and shake the earth, and spew out through the throat of a volcano, immense quantities of magma, ash, mud, scoria, pumice and vital minerals that eventually replenish the earth's surface to help sustain all life.

As I write this chapter, I have just received news of a large earthquake in central Australia, which is most unusual as Australia being the oldest continent on the planet is seldom seismically active. The report says one of the biggest earthquakes recorded in Australia has struck near an outback farm but no damage has been reported. The 6.1 magnitude earthquake was recorded near Emabella, in South Australia's far north, just before 8.30pm, local time, March 23rd 2012. Emabella is home to a few hundred indigenous Australians. The area is just south of the border with the Northern Territory, about 317 kilometres southwest of Alice Springs and 415 kilometres north of Coober Pedy, which places the epicentre fairly near the centre of the continent. The depth of the quake was recorded as 3 kilometres, which is extremely shallow. The earthquake was the biggest recorded in Australia, since a 6.3 magnitude earthquake struck off the coast of Collier Bay, on Western Australia's North Coast in 1997. Both these tremors prove how quakes can occur in the most unusual areas, which are not generally seismically active. It is understandable that there are many different estimates of the number of quakes that occur each year, the reason being that thousands of tremors are so slight they cannot be felt, let alone shake the earth above. On estimate claims that there are more than one million tremors a year, the majority of which would be extremely slight, which also supports my theory that an earthquake is an explosion of gas enriched magma, comprised of a wide variety of different elements. The magnitude of the explosion and the consequent tremor being governed by the composition and amount of magma involved, as it is being activated and propelled up and under the lithosphere where it is finally pressurized to explode; thus rupturing and shaking the surface of the earth.

The following is a summary of ancient and recent eruptions in the Asian area, beginning with the Indonesian volcano, Toba, eruption of 7200B.C., Kelut 1586, Asana, Japan 1783, Unzen, Japan 1792, Tambora, Indonesia 1815, Jalungung, Indonesia 1822, Shiviluck, Russia 1854, Awu, Indonesia 1856, Krakatoa, Indonesia 1883, Bandaisan, Japan 1883, Faal, Phillapines 1911, Merapi, Indonesia 1930, Bezymainny, Russia 1956, Kelut, Indonesia 1963, Agung, Indonesia 1963, Tolbachik, Russia 1975, Unzen, Japan 1991, Pinatubo, Phillapines 1991. Then you have constant activity of Maunoa Loa, Moana Kea and Kiluao on the Big island of Hawaii; also the ancient eruption of Taupo, New Zealand, which is quoted as happening about a third of a million years ago, when the main eruption is reported as ejecting 100 square kilometres of material, such as rock, ash and pumice over the whole of the central North Island of New Zealand, and into the provinces of Auckland, Bay of Plenty and Hawkes Bay. Vesuvius Stromboli and Etna in Italy have a long history of eruptions. The United States has actually 185 volcanoes and volcanic fields; and the biggest and deadliest of their eruptions were Crater lakes 2900B.C, Novarupta 1912, Lassen Peak 1914, St Helen's 1980, and Redoubt 1989, and Spurr 1992. One of the most volcanically active places on earth is Iceland with its increasing number of new volcanoes. Then there are the Atlantic island volcanoes of the Azores, Canary Islands, Cape Verde and Tristan de Cumpa in the South Atlanta. Then there's the Caribbean with Mount Pelee, also Mexico with many active volcanoes and finally, South America with many ancient and recent eruptions and earthquakes. With so much seismic activity around the whole globe, I find it puzzling that geologists did not pick up the source and powerful force that magma can generate to rupture and shake such wide areas of land mass. For the new scientists to have adopted the suspect idea of Wegener's theory of Continental drift, where all the continents were on one single land mass that broke up and drifted apart, is difficult to understand. The present continents and adjacent islands just do not fit. Australia, New Zealand and Indonesia do not match anywhere on the Asian coastline. Europe and the east coast of North America, plus Iceland, do not match. The North America Western Seaboard cannot be blended into Japan and the east coast of China. The whole theory is geographically impossible. It is a simple exercise to fit any shape or form with a computer. A computer can put a square peg into a round hole.

Why is it that such learned and academic people accept such unproven theories when there is so much factual evidence to the contrary? I read a ludicrous article in the Times magazine quite some years ago by one of the "new scientists". This Tectonic Plate enthusiast claimed that in 50 million years time, a slither of the Californian Coast-line around Los Angeles would become real estate up on the Alaskan Coast. Surely this guy must be suffering from some form of Seismic Syndrome Disorder!

What concerns me most is that there are people around who would believe this sort of geological nonsense.

Another seismic event that often occurs, is swarms of earthquakes happening in volatile areas, but is not followed by volcanic eruptions or large earthquakes. In the Taupo area, where the earth's crust is exceedingly thin, hot springs, mud pools and even a large thermal power station prevails. Quite some years ago, Taupo began receiving swarms of earthquakes at the rate of 100 per week, but only of small magnitude. Eventually, they all died down to the relief of the townsfolk. Rotorua, not far away, has had the same experience, but it does prove with all thermal activity in the area that active magma must be so close to the surface and gives off many explosions from time to time.

I have a son who lives in the area and he tells me you can hear the explosions at night above the noise of his television.

The whole area from the volcano Mt Ruaphehu to the White Island volcano is so volatile it could shake or erupt anytime and cause immense damage. The huge deposits of pumice and the gigantic rocks sitting upright on farmland, great distances from Lake Taupo. The ancient crater that blew out such material is proof that exploding magma can propel large quantities of material such great distances; and that has also happened all around the world. It is also concrete proof that this is the same force that ruptures and shakes the earth when a volcano is not handy to relieve some of the pressure.

There are so many basic flaws in the theory of hypothetical Tectonic Plates slipping and sliding and moving under one another as a cause of triggering earthquakes. These new scientists have selected only a few conveniently placed subductian zones as plate boundaries, yet thousands of earthquakes occur a few miles or kilometres away from the edges of those so called 'Plates", as well as many big earthquakes in the centre of them – such as Russia, China, India, Turkey, Iran, the huge Pacific Ocean and North America. Most important of all, there is no accounting for where the immense force and energy comes from that raises sea beds, coast lines and transforms the landscape, as it shakes and pulverises the surface of the earth as if it were so much paper.

There is no accounting for the cause of so many after shakes, yet my explanation accounts for every single one of them, large or small.

There is also no indication of what is replacing where the suspect plates have come from as the earth is fortunately still covered in crust. The plate scientists also claim that the Pacific Plate is moving in two opposite directions at the same time, without parting in the middle, which to me as only an amateur geologist, is geologically impossible, making their whole theory unscientific. Science is accurate, classified knowledge found in fact. The theory of Tectonic Plates is not based on fact, as there is no proof. Like some strange religions, it has to be believed. Like Global warming, it is one giant hoax!

A PLANET OUT OF CONTROL

Chapter 10

It was March 1924, in the province of Hawkes Bay, situated on the east Coast of the North Island of New Zealand. It had been raining heavily in the back country where there was a cloud burst in the small mill settlement of Puketitiri, where two sawmills operated cutting down indigenous forest for the construction of houses in the towns of Napier and Hastings. The Tutaekuiri River with its headwaters in the Kaweka Ranges near the mill settlement, could not cope with the excess water and by the time the river reached the plains, the stop banks at Guppy Road broke exactly opposite O'Shaunessay's home, which had been evacuated. It disintegrated with the huge force of the water which spread over the whole countryside. That was on a Friday night and next morning the rain began to ease with just intermittent showers. We were three little boys, living in a quiet street, in the small village of Taradale. Jim and Tom Gardiner were two brothers living not far from my home, which was separated from their property by two large fields where a small herd of dairy cows grazed, owned by the local storekeeper.

Jim was not quite four years old while his brother Tom was my age, seven years old. My name being Jim too, I was known as "Big Jim". Even though I was small too, but bigger than Tom's brother, so he called him 'Little Jim". By Saturday afternoon, when the rain eased off, with the sun trying to shine, the three of us, in our respective homes, had been longingly looking out our windows at the huge sheets of surface water in the fields that separated our houses, begging our parents for permission to play in that water. As odd showers were still continuous, permission was not granted, until suddenly the sun burst through and we saw Tom and Little Jim heading for the puddles, barefooted with short trousers rolled up, running at high speed through all the surface water. At last I was granted permission to join them and to the great amusement of both sets of parents, we ran and ran one end of the field to the other, seeing who could make the biggest splash. March is autumn down under and the ground temperature was still warm, making the venture most pleasant. We finally ran out of breathe and Tom and I began discussing the huge flood and all the lower countryside being covered by over a foot of water. Tom and I must have mentioned God several times in our discussion. How such a gigantic event could have happened when suddenly Little Jim interrupted.

"Who is this God bloke you two keep talking about?" he enquired. Tom looked at me with his mouth open. We were both horrified. Tom and I had both been to Sunday school and to speak of God as a "bloke" was unheard of. "Bloke" is an Australian name for just an ordinary, run of the mill, regular male person, similar to an American 'guy' or a British, 'Chap" or "fellow". To call God a 'bloke' made Tom and me feel really bewildered and upset. Tom felt as Jim's older brother, it was his place to put the little chap straight.

"I'll tell you who he is," he explained with an authorative air, "He is the boss of the whole wide world" and he gestured with a circle as wide as his arms could enable him and looked at me for approval which I nodded in support. Little Jim thought for a while then burst out.

"Well, I'll tell you two something," he replied in his baby talk, "He's not the boss of me! And he ran off down through the puddles, laughing his head off. Tom and I looked at each other in horror; we were dumbfounded at Little Jim's outburst. It really spoilt our afternoon!

When I went home and told my parents, they laughed and laughed at the episode which puzzled me even more. I have since thought, why this little boy, just fresh from God would, question and defy this great power that controls life.

The Gardiners moved away from our district soon after the flood and I really missed them as we were great playmates despite little Jim's misunderstanding of the divine power. I often wondered how they fared in life and if little Jim ever found cosmic consciousness, after all Tom and I were only trying to teach him the benefits and power from doing good and the negative results of evil. In those days of the 1920's, there were no burglaries and just one murder per year in the whole country.

My mother used to walk to the village on the dark winter nights every Tuesday to change her library books, a distance of a kilometre. You could not do that today as you would either be robbed or raped. It is safer in the city of Beijing, China at one o'clock in the morning than my town today, soon after dark.

When I was a boy, you would not dream of locking your doors or closing all of the windows if you left the house. People are being robbed, raped and murdered during daylight hours and by young people too, which is so hard to explain.

I recently read in our daily paper, where 200 young primary school children, throughout the whole country, were banned from school for physical violence, abuse and throwing chairs at the teachers. All brought about by inept politicians legislating new laws banning smacking of children and enabling youngsters to take legal action against their parents.

The domestic violence and gross child abuse to babies including many murders of little ones, has not abated one iota because the crimes against infants especially babies, are committed in dysfunctional households by parents either on drugs or alcohol and never by responsible parents who care so much about their offspring, they are not afraid to discipline them for their own good. The switch my mother put around my legs, the strap I received at primary school, and the cane I received at secondary school, all helped to make me a better responsible human being and I am grateful for that discipline that brought me into line.

I recall reading in the Saturday Evening Post, many years ago, a report of an 18 year old young man in a USA city being sentenced to the electric chair for first degree murder. His mother sat in the courtroom sobbing her heart out... When the judge pronounced the death sentence, he asked the unfortunate lad if he had anything to say. The youth turned to his mother and shouted, "Why didn't you thrash me and give me hidings like all the other boys?" The poor woman sobbed louder realizing that she had spoiled the lad beyond reason. However, I believe there are more ways than violence to punish children. For example; I bought all my four boys a new bike for Christmas when they became responsible enough in my estimation to ride our local roads. One of my boys left his nice new machine out in the rain all night, so I explained he would be penalized for such lack of care for his bike. I informed him he would have to travel to school in the bus for a week. I could not help feeling sorry for him as the bantering he received from the other children on the bus was worse than any hiding, but he learned his lesson and looked after his new cycle for ever, with loving care. I never ever knew until years later, when my daughters were well into adulthood, that my wife had kept a strap in the kitchen drawer and when my girls used to see her reach for the strap, they knew she meant business! My children were so lucky to have parents that knew how to concentrate a tremendous amount of love in a mix of the correct amount of discipline. My only brother who was four years older than I was, a school teacher, (before he lost his life in the Pacific Theatre of the 2nd World War), and I was told several years later that he never used a strap on his pupils. In fact, he finished up giving his strap away to one of his pupils who funnily enough had it used on him from the next teacher. I often wondered to this very day, how he coped and what was his formula for maintaining good behaviour in the classroom. I only received the cane once in high school. It was customary for the whole class to stand up when the master entered the room, however, on this one day; I had dropped my pencil on the floor. I was bending down under my desk searching for it when I was called out for six of the best for not standing up immediately the master had entered the room.

With many children today, there is a complete lack of respect. As a fairly large potato producer, we often employed young lads to help with the harvest and when we were to open up a new block to dig with a harvester, we used to strike out the middle of the crop with a two row digger to be able to accommodate the larger machine which needed space. In picking up the tubers from the two row digger, we worked two pickers to a bag; and a young lad who had just started with us worked with me to learn what not to put in the bag as I was extremely fussy as to what I sold having printed bags giving a money back guarantee. Explaining to the new lad what not to put in the bag and the defects he would encounter and what should be discarded, we started to fill the bag when suddenly he exclaimed to me, "Do you mind if I call you Jim?" I looked at him with astonishment and said," Stand up. Now look here, I have grandchildren a lot older than you and if you do not show me a little respect, I'll have you clicking your heels and saluting me all the way down the row." Do you know, that lad bought me a big box of chocolates for Christmas, before I could give him one, which I usually did for all the young lads who worked for us? I asked, "What's this for?"

"Oh well, you have been so kind to me and taught me so much."

The poor lad was from a dysfunctional family and must have had it really tough without a dad.

Another boy who was such a little fellow, yet my son showed him how to drive the big tractor that pulled the harvester. This little lad looked so small sitting up there on such a high seat, which was not dangerous and was the easiest job on the machine, as the tractor had to be driven in the lowest gear with the throttle well back otherwise the crew on the sorting table could not cope with the crop. He loved the job so much and he earned and saved so much money, he was devastated when his mother told him that they would be shifting away. He told her bluntly that he would not be going - he just loved working with my eldest son, Barry and did not want to miss all the work. His mother asked him where he would stay if he did not come with the rest of the family. Now on our property there was a huge storage shed that housed many tractors, implements and large bins we stored pumpkins in. His reply to his mother was, "Oh, Barry will let me sleep in the empty bin in the shed." He was heartbroken not to be able to continue to work with us. I often wondered what became of him.

We used to produce a large area of potatoes up at our back country farm that was situated in the volcanic ash country from the Taupo eruption. It was 26 miles from where our home headquarters were stationed and we took two big trucks that could hold seven tons of potatoes each, up to the farm every day.

The two trucks left early with the crew and I followed in a small utility truck. One day, one the way up to the farm, I came across a young boy walking in the same direction, I was heading. I pulled up and offered him a lift. He gladly accepted and as I drove I asked him, "Did you miss the bus?"

"Oh, no," he replied, "I am not on the way to school; I am going up to see my uncle at Rissington." Rissington is a small settlement halfway to my farm. When we reached his uncle's place, he said, "I don't think he is home." "What will you do?" I asked. "I don't know" he replied. "Would you like to come up to our farm and help on the harvester, digging potatoes?" I asked and he readily agreed. Of course he had no lunch or smoko refreshments, however, he finished up with the best lunch of all as each of us, including my helpers, gave him a sandwich each, a banana and an orange. He had the best variety of all and at the end of the day, a pay cheque to boot; and he was able to travel back early in the first truck to leave. As my driver of the first truck was nearing its destination, he enquired of the lad where he would like to be dropped off, to which he replied, he didn't want to get home and would sooner be taken to his Auntie's place which was near our home. It turned out the unfortunate lad's parents had just separated and when I picked him up he was actually running away from home as he was so upset with the breakup. It so happened the next day at school, he gave a morning talk on his precious day's events and how he had spent the day harvesting potatoes with the nice people who shared their lunch with him and then paid him a cheque for his help. Little did he realize that a girl classmate of his was my granddaughter who upon arriving home from school, unfolded the unfortunate story. It is so sad for children, especially when they are young, to lose a parent through a marriage break-up as it is the children who suffer the most. While the boy in a family needs a father most and girls need a mother, but most of all, the boy and girl really need them both. Happy and contented is the household where both parents love one another until death do they part; but the praise must go to the lady of the home, most of all because she plays the greatest part in holding a family together.

The hands that rock the cradle are the greatest heroes or in this case heroines, but they are the least honoured. Most mothers are God's angels with a few exceptions of lost souls destroyed by unfortunate frailties of humanity where often drugs and alcohol are the culprits.

I have recently read that the USA, despite the billions of dollars it has spent, it is losing the war on drugs. I ponder the question is this retribution to the western nation who caused the Boxer Revolution in China well over a hundred years ago, when the British East India Company forced the sale of opium on the Chinese population, resulting in the Boxer Wars and a European hold on China. The chickens have finally come home to roost and our youth are paying the price. Today's drug peddlers are mass murderers, destroyers of souls, if not lives.

Alcohol and opiates may sooth and placate, but in the end destroy the mind and body. A young female's body is unsuited to the consumption of alcohol; it is not designed to take such punishment. The consumption of alcohol and binge drinking by the youth of today, are drafts to be paid at maturity. Our hospitals are stretched today not only with the elderly, they are being taken care of in elderly rest homes, but our physciatric youth problems, accidents from drunk drivers and those on drugs.

Despite the fact that most of us were broke, we were far better off in the great depression of the thirties. There were no burglaries, few murders, you left your windows open all day and all, nights and you never thought of locking you doors. The only risk was the odd swagger, a drifter type of man who dossed down in shearers quarters on sheep stations at night after he had trudged the highway on foot, bludging a meal here and there, carrying his bed roll or swag on his back, hence the name 'swagger'. Swaggers were fairly harmless, but they used to frighten the children in those times although they were mostly not to be feared.

The depression taught us all that it was far easier to live with adversity than prosperity. Adversity causes you to struggle and try harder to survive. It builds character and strengthens will power; it may prove also the theory of natural selection and the survival of the fittest. The depression taught you the value of money simply because there just wasn't any. It also taught you to be kind to one another, to help each other.

I remember my dad coming home one day from work just before he lost his job. He had been given a huge kingfish by a workmate and he called me to come and deliver sections of this huge fish, he began cutting up. "Here, he said, "take this piece down to the vicarage". Childlike I asked," Why are you giving the first piece to the parson?"

"Because they give the whole street apples from their large home orchard," he replied. That is where we learnt reciprocation, be kind, help others, especially those that help others as well as those who are unable to do so.

The 1931 earthquake put a lot of people back to work, especially bricklayers with all the fallen chimneys, but the slump hit hard, 1932, 1933,1934 were the worst years, with relief workers only getting three days a week on the dole. There was no actual productive work for these people, just chopping weeds on the footpath and roads.

On Fridays, my father and Bill Hamilton, an old work carpenter, had the task of cutting up sheep carcasses for distribution among these relief workers, as they hardly had enough money to buy food let alone pay rent. I remember well there were just two butchers in our village and the last one to start up went bung (that is bankrupt). I bought his 1923 Dodge, high sided, van in which he used to pick his meat up in for 4Pounds – or in today's currency $8.00. It had no lights; horn, windscreen wipers and a hopeless gear box, if you missed the first change when you took off, you had to start again. However, it was just what we needed for deerstalking, pig hunting and duck shooting to put food on the table.

When my father lost his job in 1932, he exclaimed, "Oh well, you will not catch me going on the dole, I am going down to the post and purchase some fish from George Lovell, an old Cornishman from England, who owned a large trawler, the Ohinemuri". My dad bought large bundles of what we called, Round fish, Snapper, Tarakihi, Groper, Gurnard and flat fish, Soles and Flounder. The round fish was two and a halfpenny a pound, while the flat fish was sixpence per pound. It all had been gutted, but not scaled and it was threaded on hearing string to make up a large bundle which was all weighed at the time of purchase.

My parents owned a 3 seater 1928 Dodge and my father converted the boot so it could hold all the fish. My brother, who had passed his matriculation exam, after four years at high school, could not obtain a position teaching as the government had stopped five year old children starting school, to try and save money as the country was destitute. I had left high school towards the end of my first year as a result of the slump and also my desire to go on the land to work. I was only getting casual work picking fruit, picking of potatoes and odd days in a Chinese market garden at three shillings a day. Therefore my father and brother and I journeyed over to Hasting twice a week, Tuesday, and Friday to sell door to door. I would knock on each door, "Good morning Madam, any fish today?" "No thank you," would often be the reply. Undaunted, I would reel off the varieties we had available, and then sadly the lady of the house would reply, "Sorry, sonny, I have no money."

Then at last a sale, one shilling's worth of Gurnard, the cheapest fish we sold and the wonderful lady said, "If you go around to the front door, you may make another sale!" That was what it was like in those hard times, two families living in one house and sharing amenities; perhaps a young married couple living in a tent in the back garden too. Such were the hard times in those slump years.

We often had fish over that we could not sell and my father would stop in an orchard area on the way home and say to me, "Jim, go into that orchard and see if you can swap some fish for some apples."

A tall man answered the knock on the door, Mr Melling was his name; and he looked at me suspiciously asking me what I wanted.

"Care to exchange some of this lovely fish for some apples?" I asked. He readily agreed. Orchardists had been hit hard by the slump and could not sell their fruit. He finished up giving me a bushel of lovely juicy Sturmer apples, worth about two shillings worth of groper.

My brother and I worked on the fish run for our parents for our keep, there was never any thought of payment, we were doing it to survive, as the fish run could afford no wages. The other days of the week, we were able to find odd jobs for other necessities like clothes. The local church could not afford an organist, so my brother who was an experienced piano player and had played since he was seven years old, played the organ for free right throughout the slump. In those early childhood days, we had always been given a one penny piece to put in the plate for Sunday school and a silver three pence piece if we went to church. Imagine my surprise when I took my youngest daughter to church one Sunday, when she was holidaying with me and I asked how much do we put in the plate these days, and she said, "twenty dollars!" I had forgotten inflation and yes, I had not been to church for some time, as Sunday was out busiest day in my market garden. We supplied most of the country's markets for the Monday sale or people would not have fresh vegetables to eat. It also enabled me to donate $1000.00 towards a new roof for the church, and seven thousand dollars to my daughter's parish as they could not afford to keep their new preacher, if they had not raised the funds.

My father seldom went to church, but I did find out when I was older, that he played a very important part in the annual church fair. In the vicarages large garden, there was a huge stand of tall bamboo and there was a narrow track into the centre of the growth and a small cave-like clearing therein. In the centre of this dark clearing, unbeknown to me, of course, sat my father as Father Christmas where all the doting mothers would take their little ones to visit Father Christmas. How my father must have chuckled when I was a little wide eyed child, listening to me tell him what I wanted for Christmas. When I was much older and no longer visited the cave, I was still unaware it was my dad. I must have been 30 years of age before they told me! By that time, I had children of my own entering that dark mysterious wonderland. Dad had since retired from his pleasant task.

When I look back on the good old days, bad days and compare them with the present troubled times of so many nations and countries, living so far beyond their means, thousands protesting and screaming in their streets for the removal of their leaders of government, countries like Greece having to be bailed out a second time and denouncing any austerity measures, I realise that these good old, bad days were really not that bad after all.

I remember an important dignitary visiting our country a few years ago and on perceiving the great welfare state we had institutionalised in our country explained we would be better off, but we were worse off. Many of us would now agree as we are sinking fast under the excess of welfare. One of the world's greatest statesman Lee Kuan Yew from Singapore, on visiting New Zealand, exclaimed, "I can tell you right away what is wrong with your country, you are farming children!". He is right, we are paying young people to have children, single parents, the unmarried are all on the band wagon and the country has to borrow billions to keep it up. When Michael Joseph Savage became Prime Minister in 1935 and began to put the country back to work at the end of the great depression, he did not mean for or the social security to become an industry. He meant it to help those in need, today it's our biggest growth industry. The whole world is sinking under the weight of welfare, and as a result countries are not faring well. Bailouts are the order of the day, The IMF and world banks cannot go on bailing out countries like Greece, Spain, Portugal and Ireland forever, these countries like my own, New Zealand, are going to have to learn not to live beyond their income.

These ailing countries, including mine, have been living it up for so long they cannot cope with austerity. At present the whole world's eyes are on the USA and how she is going to cope with her mounting debt. The United States of America is really suffering from an overdose of 60 years of continuous prosperity that has suddenly been halted by the effects of globalization. The jobs she hopes to re-establish have gone to China and India. The 2008 collapse of the housing market caused by irresponsible banking, fraudulent companies, and the weasels in Wall Street, who have all been bailed out by socialism to America, that great bastion of private enterprise and capitalism.

For a while, it looked as if capitalism was under threat, one could almost hear Karl Marx in the background whispering, "What did I tell you!" however, taxpayers from main street came to the rescue, but tragically the banks and fraudsters were bucking the regulations that may have prevented it happening again. That is one great problem with capitalism, while it rewards the entrepreneur, the hard workers and the risk takers; it is also tragically prone to the greedy, the fraudulent, the profiteers, and irresponsible bank and bond traders. Remember what President Elect Clinton fumed at, at a preliminary meeting of his financial team when he was querying them on balancing the budget and they exclaimed that perhaps there would be a possibility of working with bond trader to this end. The President Elect shouted, "Do you mean to tell me my re-election depends on so few Bond traders which make me wonder why trillions of dollars spin daily around the world in wanton unproductive speculation just for the sheer profit of few financial parasites. These predators have contributed zero to the economies of the world while millions of hardworking, productive taxpayers keep their prospective economies afloat, have to struggle to survive. It is this unproductive, fraudulent side of capitalism that makes people look to socialism for a solution. People all over the world are concerned at what is happening to this once great nation, the United States of America, the nation that saved Europe from the Nazis and all the Pacific Nations, including China and India from the Japanese. The nation that is always the first to come to the aid of countries hit by natural disasters. The most generous nation in the world is now in deep financial trouble. Centuries ago Nero fiddled while Rome burned. Today, congressmen and women are playing politics, while the nation's fiscal policies remain unsolved. President Obama inherited two wars that he cannot win, a colossal debt which he had to increase to prevent a world-wide depression and worst of all, a nation that is so used to living beyond its means.

Perhaps America should borrow Angela Merkle, the de-facto president of Europe, for a few years to get their country back on track. Hitler would be green with envy if he could come back and see what Germany has achieved without firing a shot! He would realise his greatest mistake was that he put Germanys' male population into uniforms instead of overalls.

Despite all the financial chaos which will echo around the world, if America does not reform and regulate their banks and make some changes to what appears to be a dysfunctional political system. You cannot help admiring their willingness to air their dirty washing. The British sweep theirs under the carpet, the Russians clobber the media and make out nothing is happening, while America bares all, perhaps that maybe a sign for some hope. Let us all hope that is so, because the world needs a strong America. They saved us twice and they just might have to do it again. It must be exasperating for financial stalwarts like Paul Volcker and down to earth astute ladies like Elizabeth Warren who are wide awake to the cause of the current debt crisis, but can do little about it as it would hamper the fraudsters, free all the irresponsible banking and the world's greatest casino, Wall Street; that knows nothing about productivity.

The corporate greed, that almost brought down capitalism, that had to be bailed out by socialism, is still alive and well. Any move by Obama to control, eliminate or regulate to prevent a repetition of the 2008 meltdown is opposed by the Republicans, which indicates that the G.O.P. must be in favour of fraud. It is all so confusing the President may be on the wrong track, as bailouts are only a temporary injection to the patient, like giving an intoxicated person another bottle of whiskey to prop them up. Parties, Democrats and Republicans keep harping on about Jobs! Jobs, Jobs! When they both know the jobs have gone to China and India.

Here is an example; I am a capitalist and a small millionaire, although I had no desire to become one. I just wanted to produce nutritious, flavoursome, horticultural produce with the edible characteristics that satisfied my customers as I always considered the consumer my boss.

The first John Deere I bought was made in Germany, so was my second, third and fourth. Recently I traded in my front end loader John Deere for the latest model, and for the first time in my life, the price had come down. My first John Deere front end loader cost me $62,000, twenty years ago. My new one, with the great improvements, was landed on my property for $49,000; and the agent gave me $20,000 as a trade-in for my old one. I found it hard to conceal my delight! Better still; the agent assured me it was made in the USA which pleased me no end, as I had faith in the American machinery. As my first new truck was a Ford V8, and then a Ford 39 car, second hand, then a Ford 1946 Mercury followed by a 1957 Ford Custom Line, then a 1962 Pontiac, all gave me wonderful service for my large family. However, when my chief helper was looking over my new tractor, he discovered a small plate under the radiator that read, "Assembled in India." No wonder the price had dropped! Cheap labour! American jobs gone for good – how does the USA expect to get them back? The Politicians are fanning the air with baloney! I will be surprised if any political party in the USA can reverse the situation, where over 60 years of prosperity that ended in corporate greed, corruption, bribery, irresponsible banking, fraud, plus the Wall Street casino and globalisation has undermined the American economy, God help us all if she goes down!

The politicians of the USA had better take those "Occupy Wall Street" Protestors seriously, despite the few weirdoes and rabble rousers among their ranks. Their number is likely to grow by an influx of genuinely concerned Main Street supporters who have had enough of the political skulduggery that is rife in the USA.

The whole world's economic situation is balanced on a knife edge!

Perhaps China would be willing to come to the aid of the Euro zone bailout. It would prove just how vital the European and USA economies are to the World trade. The big question is, if the banks are prepared to write off 50% of the Greek debt, will they not encourage them to forget about mending their ways, remembering that there are also other Euro member countries teetering on the brink of fiscal instability? If they collapse, the one trillion Euros fund will not be enough!

The wisest economists in the world cannot solve this world wide problem simply because it has not a lot to do with economics. It is all to do with human behaviour, which unfortunately defies analysis, the best psychiatrist's in the world cannot explain the frailties of human behaviour. Bailouts are only an aesthetic measure and a temporary one at that.

President Obama's bailouts did not punish the perpetrators, they even benefited by receiving bonuses for the main street tax funded windfall. Somewhere along the line there has to be some pain for us all to bear. Countries, all countries, including my own little neck of the woods are going to have to learn to live within their income. I always taught my children that it is not how much money you have got that counts, it is what you do with what you have got that matters. Money does not have to be the route of all evil; it is how you handle money that counts in the long run.

Let me give you an example, a young lad up North won a huge Lottery prize, about a million dollars and still applied for the dole. The lady at the office explained that he was no longer eligible for such a handout while he was so well off. The poor guy panicked, he tried to get rid of his winnings by giving it away, he bought cars for his family etc, etc. But it was still not enough. He just did not know how to handle such a windfall. He could have put it on deposit for 5% interest and he would not have had to work; but no, he blew it because it was too much at once for the poor guy to cope with. He had never experienced a slump – he was a product of the welfare system and of good times.

However, the best example of all is an article I read in a business magazine, in a certain town in South Africa. A family who resided there had a large vegetable garden and at the end of their section was a large clump of tall trees where a colony of storks was resting. One day a young stork fell out of one of the nests and landed in the garden. The children of the family picked it up and took it to their parents and asked them if they could keep it as a pet. The father was not agreeable, as he explained that the children would have to dig up worms every day to feed the young chick. The children gave their father a hard time – promising they would only be too willing to keep the chick well fed. Finally, the father consented. The children called the stork "Major" and it became a great pet. Then one day when the children were at school and Major was sitting on the handle of a fork, which was used to dig up worms for him, he heard the cries of a flock of other storks overhead, heading north for the winter. Feeling the call of the wild, Major took off and joined the migratory flock on route northwards. When the children came home from school and found Major had vanished, they were heartbroken. Their Dad's only consolation was that it was bound to happen as the call of the wild was natural for Major to join his fellow storks. Three days went by and lo and behold, when the children arose the next morning, there was Major sitting on the fork in the garden, looking utterly famished, squawking his head off for worms. What had evidently happened, was when the flock of storks had alighted in a field on the way north for a snack of worms and grubs, they simply told poor old Major to get his own. No one had taught Major how to fend for himself. Undaunted, he kept up with the flock, but at each stopover, no one fed Major- all the other storks were too busy fending for themselves. There was only one solution. Major left the flock and flew back to the safety of a provided meal, much to the children's delight. Major had been the victim of welfare, but was now back on track. The lesson to be learnt from this episode is that all wild life brings up its offspring to fend for themselves, which not only insures their survival, but the continuation of the species. Whereas, quite often humans are reluctant to wean their children and sometimes molly coddle them away past adolescence, denying them the chance of standing on their own.

How often have we seen a young lad who has just lost his dad in an accident, take over the responsibility of the family at the going down of the sun, to the dawn the next day, become a real man overnight?

In 1970, my wife and I went on a New Zealand Fruit Growers trip of the World. I myself called on markets in every city we visited as I was deeply involved in our own countries growers' federation. I befriended the president of a large USA city market, who had fought in the Pacific War, pushing back the Japanese. He came home at the end of hostilities, borrowed $500.00 off his mother in law; and with his gratuity bought an ex-army truck and hawked fruit and vegetables around his local township; and eventually became president of the city's largest wholesale fruit and produce market. As we swapped stories of our experiences in the industry, I enquired if he had any family in the business. His bluntness shocked me when he exclaimed. "No, my son's a bum, he's Flower Power, and I had to kick him out!" How sad for a man who fought on Tarawa, came through it all, to come home and work 18 hours a day to become so prosperous that it destroyed his son. I have seen the same disaster happen in my own little country. Prosperity can sometimes be the cause of failure and yet again, failure as in my case, can be the mother of prosperity.

A Brigadier friend of mine who fought in the Middle East during the Second World War, informed me that sometimes when they were choosing an officer to lead the troops into a difficult impending battle, they would say, "Let's choose someone who has recently suffered a recent defeat" It would really pay off. Winning all the time can be dangerous in sport, business or war; complacency can set in and be so devastating. Success can only be achieved by constant vigilance. Hardship, adversity, setbacks not only bring you back to earth, they build character, prepare you to take knocks, ensure your chance of survival in an over –competitive world that is always going to be a rat race. After the extravagances of the roaring twenties, when America really "made Woopie", it all came tumbling down in the market crash of 1930's. President Roosevelt brought the country through it with his "new deal". Then victory in the Second World War, followed by the

Cold War, ended in the collapse of Communism. Now, we still have even greater threats - the war on terrorism, the international financial crisis and the population explosion.

We have now reached seven billion people and another billion to be added every 13 years, according to experts. The planets resources are already stretched, deforestation and diversification is rampant; some experts inform us that fresh water is going to be short. There is no question we had plundered the earth's natural resources. Every so often some nutter predicts the end of the world will happen upon a certain date; but when the sun rises and the sun goes down on that day; and the Hang Sung rises or falls, Wall Street plays its casino like game; and the deficit increases but life goes on. When the crackpots talk about the end of the world, they really mean the end of this civilisation. That is quite a likely certainty, but nobody knows whether it will be several volcanoes belching enough debris into the atmosphere to blot out the sun or an asteroid that could have an even more devastating effect.

This reminds me of an old story of a Father Flanagan who was walking down the street in one of the suburbs of Dublin one day, when he observed Patrick O'Rielly methodically digging over his vegetable garden. The priest observed him for a while and then asked," Patrick, what would you do if I told you the world was going to come to an end tomorrow?" Pat stopped digging, took out his pipe, tapped it on the handle of his spade and replied, "Just keeping digging, Father, Just keep digging."

That is what we all have to do, just keep digging or just keep on doing the good work that keeps things ticking over; and try to eliminate the unproductive, negative things in life. During the 94 years I have lived on this wonderful planet, I have witnessed the fall of National Socialism as practised by the Nazi's, the end of the 70 odd year experiment in Communism as tried by Russia; the near collapse of capitalism on an International scale; and in 2008 when banks, business and financial institutions had to be bailed out by their respective governments with taxpayers money.

I never ever thought I would see the day capitalism would have to be propped up by socialism! We can only hope that China with her hybrid experiment of Communists for the people and capitalism for the business does not succumb to the same type of Hill Billy banking as recently practised by the western economies who we are still told are not out of the woods.

With practically the whole world in a political and financial mess, with terrorists and protestors everywhere, with the Middle east a continuous powder keg of unrest, perhaps humanity has reached the stage where we are like the seven billion Lemmings fast tracking to oblivion! Who knows! The only thing that is certain is that nature is the boss and although humanity is the only form of life on earth that defies nature, nature will win in the end, as it is natural that all forms of life on earth have their periods of birth, infancy, youth, and maturity and finally decay.

Kingdoms, Dynasties, Empires, Civilisation are no exceptions – perhaps it is time for Mother Earth to think about a clean slate.

AVERTING ANOTHER WORLD WAR

Chapter 11

I wish to acknowledge A.J.P. Taylor and his book "The First World War" for the information in this chapter, marked with an asterix.

When Arch Duke Franz Ferdinand, the heir to the Monarchy of the Hapsburgs, married Countess Sophie Chotek on June 28th 1900, little did he realise he had set the date of both their deaths. Their wedding day was a sad and subdued ceremony as Sophie Chotek being a mere Countess did not come with the permitted degrees of an Imperial Habsburg dynasty. As a result Franz Ferdinand had to sign away the rights of any children born of the marriage. Their wedding day actually set the fuse to the First World War. Franz Ferdinand was a brutal, obstinate man, impatient with opposition, but he had one redeeming feature, he adored and loved his wife. It irked him that he could never share his splendours and she could never ever accompany him or sit by his side in public occasions. However, there was one loophole. As Field Marshal and Inspector-General of the Austria Hungarian army, his wife could enjoy the recognition of his rank when he was acting in a military capacity. Hence the Arch Duke decided to inspect the army in Bosnia. In its capital, Sarajevo, he and his wife could ride in an open carriage, side by side, on 28th June, the anniversary of their wedding day. Thus, ironically for love, did the Arch Duke go to his death. Bosnia and its sister province, Herzegovina were recent Hapsburg acquisitions. Formerly Turkish and scene of many rebellions, they had been administered by Austria Hungary since 1878, annexed only in 1908. The inhabitants were southern Slavs or Croats; and many of the younger ones were resentful at having been brought under the Hapsburgs. Instead of being allowed to join Serbia, their national state. Patriotic young men conspired together and made unsuccessful attempts to assassinate Hapsburg officials. When it became known of the Arch Duke's impending visit, half a dozen young grammar school boys decided to have a shot at him. They received encouragement from a Serb society that provided them with some crude weapons. On June 28th, the Arch Duke and his wife drove into Sarajevo, but initially the plot went wrong. One young conspirator failed to draw his revolver, another felt sorry for the Arch Duke's wife and went home and a third threw his bomb but missed. When the Arch Duke reached the town hall, he was furious; his wife's treat had been ruined, so he decided to drive straight out of town, without notifying his chauffeur. He took a wrong turning, then stopped the car and reversed. Garilo Princip, one of the students in the plot saw before him the stationery car. He stepped onto the running board of the car and killed the Arch Duke with one shot, then aimed at the escort in the front seat, but hit the Arch Duke's wife sitting in the back. She too, died almost immediately. The assassination was far more than a crime, it was a challenge, and it was a challenge to Austria/Hungary as ruler of Bosnia. It was a challenge to her prestige as a great power. Historians from here on have never been able to agree what went wrong. Britain and Germany were on friendly terms as was Germany and France, it was generally assumed that there would be an alliance with Britain, France and Germany, as all three were more concerned with the Russian Colossus. German Industrialists did not want war; they were doing so well they knew full well that Germany would soon become the leading power in Europe through sheer economic strength. Why spoil it with war? Some historians argued that the Kiel Canal had only just been widened for German dreadnoughts in July 1914 and that German army was at the height of its superiority. Many claimed that Europe was a powder keg awaiting a spark to ignite it. Was the assignation that spark?'The real cause has never been made clear as nowhere was there conscious determination to provoke war. However, statesmen began to miscalculate, they used the instruments of bluff and threat which had proved effective on previous occasions - this time things went wrong. The deterrent on which they relied, failed to deter and the statesmen became the prisoners of their own weapons. The great armies accumulated to provide peace and security, carried the nations to war by the own weapons. Austria having had precious trouble with Serbia decided to take a strong stand. They looked to Germany for support which was forthcoming. They were promised German backing if Russia supported Serbia. Although this was not a decision for war as threats had brought prestige and peaceful decisions before. Germany's rulers assumed that the same would happen again. The Austrians tried to find some proof that the Serbian Government decision was involved with the assassination, however, none was found. On the 23rd July, the Hungarian Government sent an ultimatum to Serbia, intending to humiliate her. The Serbs accepted with enough reservation to save a little prestige. Austria Hungary immediately broke off relations, followed by a declaration of war. It was really a diplomatic manoeuvre although seemingly a most violent one, yet the Austria Hungarian Army could not be ready for many weeks. This is when Russia became involved as the protector of the Slave States in the Balkans, beside not allowing Serbia to be humiliated, Russia had to consider that, if Germany and Austria (Hungary dominated the Balkans) they would control Constantinople and the Straits through which most of Russia's trade, therefore Russia's motive was security and survival.

The Russians did not want war, even though she mobilized, it was really to keep her standing in the diplomatic conflict. Russia merely wanted to show that when Austria Hungary threatened, she could threaten too. Bluff after bluff was piled on top of another, it seemed to be getting out of hand. Germany assumed that what mobilization meant was; either they had to stop Russia's mobilization at once by threat of war, or they had to start a war, also at once. Germany sent an ultimatum demanding demobilization within twelve hours. The Russian's refused, so on the 1st August, Germany declared war on Russia and two days later against France, with hardly an attempt at excuse.

As the frontier between France and Germany was heavily fortified on both sides, there was no chance of a quick victory there. To the north of it lay Belgium making a sort of funnel through which the German armies could pass and be in a better position to attack the French. On 2nd August, the Germans demanded a free passage through Belgium.

The Belgium's refused. This refusal brought in Britain. Up into now she had hesitated being determined not to be drawn into the Balkan quarrel, however, Germany's demand removed all doubts and Britain declared war on Germany, the only country to do so instead of the other way around. Austria Hungary, who had started all the upheaval between the powers, was the last to get going.

Prodded by Germany, she finally declared war on Russia on 6th August. Great Britain and France were also reluctant to break off relations with Austria Hungary, but declared war against her on 10th August.

At first Socialists and Bolsheviks in every country, voted almost entirely, against the war, but were over-ruled as every nation thought they were defending their very existence, even though the method of defence was to invade someone else's territory. Consequently, six million men from all the nations involved marched into battle, most of them thinking the war would be over by Christmas. Sadly, it was to be followed by four years of deadlock where at times 250,000 Germans were thrown into battle against 250,000 allied forces in a futile fight to win or lose a few hundred yard of crated mud. The war was never fought on German soil; France and Belgium were the two countries where the war stalemated.

On Christmas Day 1914, German and British Offices fraternised, as well as troops who even played football – only photos of officers only were permitted to be taken.

On this Christmas Day in France, firing stopped on the frontline, British and German soldiers met in 'no man's land', exchanged cigarettes, gossiped and met again the next day, but were rebuked from headquarters, so firing gradually started again. The following Christmas, it was an entirely different story!

So began a war of hatred between Britain and her German cousins. Germany accused Britain of interfering in Europe by trying to prevent unification under German leadership, instead of being content with her own empire. Hatred was now in full swing. Britain was now Germany's enemy No. 1 and looked forward to her collapse. Britain on the other hand believed that they were now fighting for their very existence against their former German cousins. The king even changed his own German name to the English Windsor, which it remains to this day. Thus the conflict turned into truly Anglo- German duel which must cast doubt on the previous suspect cause of the war.

According to the well-known historical writer A.J.P. Taylor, whose book "The First World War' from which much if this information has been obtained, wrote that the young Garilo Princip who assassinated Franz Ferdinand's wife Sophie as firing the first two shots of World War 1.

If this is so, then they were the first two shots of World War 1, and this was the direct cause of the next World War. The reason being that the moment the ink dried on that document, The Treaty of Versailles, Nazism was conceived and an Austrian upstart and despot named Adolf Hitler was on his way.

However, the Treaty was far from perfect; the amount of reparation to be paid by Germany to the victors was left in the air. President Wilson's insistence on the principle of self-determination resulted in the creation of several more little states each with its own sovereignty built mostly from the ruins of Russia and Austria-Hungarian Empire, with parts contributed by the German ex empires. This new world did not give a look of permanence. Super imposed on it however, was The League of Nations, looked upon as the one gain of the war, an institution designed as the order revision of the treaties and the peaceful adjustment of international differences whenever and wherever they are.

However, the disassociation of the U.S.A. from the League and the reluctance of Britain to turn the entente into a full Anglo-French alliance, gave France uneasiness as to her future security and promised ill for the disarmament. The economic state of Europe bled white by four years of conflict and the unexpected demands by the United States, the supreme creditor of all, foreshadowed maximum efforts to make the Germans pay. Britain and France were still backing a series of futile crusades by Czarist generals against Russian bolshevism. By 1923, Britain began to doubt the efficacy of French methods of exacting payments from Germany which included taking over of capital assets. Raymond Poincare, the French Prime Minister, made proposals concerning deliveries of coal by Germany on account of reparations. The German economy collapsed with the shock. Critics in Britain and elsewhere prophesied that one day the Ruhr adventure would be costly for everyone. The young German republic tired of reparations and weakened by the loss of the Ruhr's coal production, could no longer feed herself and was almost bankrupt.

By 1923, inflation was so rampant that German marks were being baled for waste paper. Ever since the end of war, chaos reigned throughout German and the whole country became prey to the reactionary forces that prevailed. Communists tried to take over the whole country and when fighting broke out, 500 people were killed in street riots and the communist leader was executed as a result. Germanys only solution was to borrow money from the U.S.A. to pay its reparations. Meanwhile, Communists, Socialists and Nazis continued to fight for power and even though Hitler was gaoled for almost a year, he finally emerged the victor and took over from Hindenburg in 1933.

*Hitler immediately announced himself as the saviour of Europe from Bolshevism. He suppressed all oppositions and reorganised Germany along totalitarian lines. His policy was to disintegrate the world order, in which Germany being deficient in raw materials was dependant on friendly collaboration of other nations and to produce by territorial and political expansion, a greater Germany which would have absolute freedom of political action. His real aim being German dominion over

Europe. Observers misjudged him when they assumed he was just letting off hot air.

However, prior to Hitler's take-over, the U.S.A., embarrassed by the disorganisation of the trade caused by the payment of debts and reparations, built a record tariff to keep out foreign goods. Such tariffs and restrictions everywhere against their goods made it impossible for Germany to export in sufficient volume to pay her reparation debits or the interest on loans. Trade stagnation and over production ran the normal curve of the trade cycle, virtually over a precipice. The U.S.A. banking system collapsed and a worldwide slump set in. In 1932, the U.S.A. really tightened its belt, chided Europe for its extravagance and halted its loans. The whole world was now in the midst of the greatest economic depression ever known.*

The burning question is how could a bankrupt nation, Germany unable to feed herself, torn apart by political power struggles from here on in the mid 30's build a mechanised army such as the world had ever seen and an air force that astonished the world, while soup kitchens and bankruptcies predominated the rest of the world.

By 1935, Hitler had built 31 new submarines, had withdrawn Germany from the League of Nations and was marching according to Hitler's, "Suppression of Communism".

*Then the Leagues took another body blow in the east by Japan resigning from it, and thereupon conquering Manchuria and later invaded China.

At this stage Russia offered to make a German-Soviet non- aggression pact, but Hitler declined as he needed the 'Peril of Bolshevism" as an excuse for increasing armaments. In the name of German Unity, Hitler had suppressed Jews, Communists, Liberals, Catholics, Freemasons and Christians; he purged the Nazi left wing, in which large numbers including many leaders were killed. On 14th September 1934, Soviet Russia had been a pariah to the western democracies. Invited by France, it now re-joined the European Community of nations and entered the League, taking the seat previously occupied by Nazi Germany.

The move upset Berlin, and elsewhere, at this addition to the Leagues strength. In July 1934, after signing a League pact of mutual assistance with Soviet Russia and Czechoslovakia, France now aimed at signing up in a Bloc of all those Eastern European Nations willing to resist aggression. Germany was invited but Hitler declined to sign up to anything with Soviet Russia. A year later, Hitler was still refusing to join any peace pact to which Soviet Russia was a party. The League continued to condemn Germany as her armaments mounted. On 24th June 1935, a conference of Britain, France and Italy to heal differences and build up collective security took place at Stresa.

Britain made a navel pact with Germany, when nobody was looking. It was rumoured that there was a private understanding (or misunderstanding,) between Mussolini and the French Prime Minister about Abyssinia. In the autumn of 1935, protesting impatience with the League, Mussolini invaded Abyssinia, so once again the League was put to a vital test. Fifty states led by Britain, condemned the invasion and the League applied sanctions against Italy, but the League's action was fruitless. Abyssinia was conquered and Mussolini withdrew Italy from the League.

In September 1935, Nazi Germany, encouraged by the futility of the League's action to thwart the Italian invasion of Abyssinia, took advantage of the League's weakness by breaking the Treaty of Versailles to introduce conscription. It looked serious for the League. March 1936, Hitler explained that the tremendous increase in his armaments were necessary to face the increasing menace of Soviet Russia. The weakness of the League in being unable to stop Mussolini's invasion of Abyssinia, gave Hitler the cue to further break the Treaty of Versailles by re-grouping the Rhineland.* King Edward V111's reaction to this move was to inform the British Prime Minister, 'You will not touch him!" If the King of England and the politicians of both Britain and France had failed to realise the seriousness of this move, threatening the future peace of Europe, then there was at least one man who was wide awake to the danger, and left no stone unturned to make it clear. That person was a New Zealander, named David Low, a cartoonist working for a London tabloid. His cartoons were of outstanding quality, depicting Hitler in all his belligerent moves and his aggressive attitude to the rest of Europe. Low was named "Cartoonist of the Century" and his work so infuriated Hitler, that every time he was shown in Low's latest cartoon, he flew into a rage, knowing it was the truth. Low consequently became the Gestapo's number one on their hit list. Hitler even engaged the German Ambassador to Britain to approach his British counterpart to put a stop to Low's works. The cartoonist laughed off the attempt to thwart his efforts and it only made him keener and looked upon the move as a verification he was on the right track. Did the political leaders of both Britain and France really think that Hitler's crusade against the Russian Bolshevism would work in their favour?*

Hitler intended to invade Russia all right, but only when it suited him, he needed to make a stronger Germany first. It was a case of the dog bites the trainer. The burning question is though, how could Germany, a bankrupt nation, in the height of a worldwide depression, build a mechanised army and an air force such as the world had never seen, while the rest of the world was still struggling economically from the effects of the depression. It was never, ever revealed from where he obtained the finance. It is a well-known fact that the day the market crashed in October 1929, Willy Messerschmitt was in Wall Street raising money for his plane. It has also been established that many planes of Goering's air force were fitted with Roll Royce engines. Nothing unusual about these facts, I suppose. I remember my mother, who lived in the north of England, prior to1914, telling me, that in the days before WW1, Prussian military personal were often seen on local farms buying up all the horses they could, for the German cavalry. She used to recall these Germans querying owners of the horses, 'Will it stand fire?" Makes you wonder just what goes on in these circumstances. Even in our own little old country, New Zealand, I can recall the long lines of open railway wagons loaded with scrap metal all bound for Japan in the mid- thirties. All to be fired back us in the Pacific War.

So I suppose, along with the King and the politicians, we were all guilty of misjudging who the enemy really was, all except David Low. No wonder he made Hitler furious.

However, I still find it bewildering how a bankrupt country could build such an arsenal of planes, tanks, submarines, such as the world had never seen. The reason Hitler gained such support within his own country was that he put German people back to work, even though his power went to his head and finally destroyed him. His fatal mistake was he put the male population of Germans into uniforms instead of overalls. If Hitler had come back in 1960 and seen what half of his country had achieved without firing one shot, he would have been green with envy. Had he come back even more recently he would be astounded see a unified Germany, now the leading power in Europe within a European union bailing out spendthrift, bankrupt members in an effort to prevent the total European Union from collapsing.

The German economy's strength can be put down to hard work and thrift, while other members of the union overindulged on cheap credit and living beyond their means, they now expect Germany to bail them out. The only solution is for severe austerity measures otherwise the bailouts will be on going and the lesson of living within one's income will never be learnt, thus seriously affecting the future survival of the European Union.

The main reason I have recalled these tragic events leading up to WW1, when Europe and the supporting countries lost the flower of youth, was to emphasis just how easy it is for the international misunderstandings to escalate out of control by power struggles, greed, and economic failure. At the end of WW2, we witnessed the complete opposite from the Treaty of Versailles. Instead of imposing reparations, harsh penalties and humiliation, the USA and its Marshal Plan, rebuilt both Germany and Japan to such a degree, as previous stated, German is the leading economy in Europe, and I myself can no longer purchase a British Bedford or American Ford or Chevy truck. I have to choose between a Nissan and an Isuzu. My first John Deere tractor was made in Germany.

Germany and Japan lost the war but seem to have won the peace; where as Britain on the other hand, won the war but lost her empire and was so crippled financially by two world wars. She even lost the pound sterling as the world's currency to the US dollar which is now under threat as her fiscal dilemma deteriorates. Destiny sure takes some strange roads in the historical events of mankind.

What I am really concerned about is this, that if a couple of pistol shots from a young school boy terrorist, can spark an international conflagration that ends in excess of a 100 million deaths, 10 million in the first World war; over 20 million on the 1918 influenza epidemic, which was caused by the war; and the 70 million war service personnel and civilians from WW2, then noble world concerns should be the continuous threat from despotic rulers of small countries and suicidal terrorists with such a deadly arsenal at their disposal.

After the 9/11, President Bush confused, at the horror of the twin towers catastrophe, kept asking the question, 'Why do they hate us?" A Muslim school class in my country cheered when they saw the twin towers aflame on TV. They should have been ordered out of the country! What on earth are they teaching? To answer President Bush's question. Some people on this planet hate winners! The success of the USA over time as the world's largest economy causes jealousy and envy to the ignorant world that get upset by her wealth and power.

Yet the USA is the most generous country in the world, always first to send aid to countries stricken by natural disasters. The USA saved Europe twice from German military excursions and also the whole of the Pacific, including China and India for Japanese invasion. Yet the people have short memories. As an example, my eldest son and I caught up with an American couple playing golf one day. They kindly invited us to join them. It was at the time of the big ANZUS row between the USA and New Zealand over banning the visits of nuclear powered US ships to New Zealand. At the time we had an anti- American socialist government in our country that were on a trendy, "Ban the Bomb" crusade, by a then popular Prime Minister. My reply to the invitation to this kindly American was, "Well, really the way our Prime Minister is treating you country after saving us from the Japanese, my son and I should really carry you and your wife's golf bags for the remainder of the round". He laughed and responded, 'Oh, that's ok, if you don't want us, not to worry." So we joined them and had an enjoyable last few holes of golf.

On reaching the club house he said, 'Now can I buy you a drink?"

"No way", I replied. "You never let us pay for anything when we visited your country, so I'm dammed if I am going to let you pay when you visit ours!"

We all had a great old chat and it turned out he used to fly transport planes from Guam to Vietnam.

The point I would like to make clear, is that at the end of WW2 in the Pacific, Australia and New Zealand pressured the USA to form a defence force to be ready in case hostilities ever broke out again. That is how ANZUS came about and because US had to keep up with USSR's nuclear arsenal and not be caught unarmed as before, our inept Government turned them away.

Those American sailors were sleeping alongside those reactors, keeping our country safe and we were too miserable to give the poor guys a bit of liberty in our ports.

While just across the Tasman, Australia also under the control of a socialist government and with a Prime Minister who has previously been the President of Australia's unions, acted quite the opposite to New Zealand. Bob Hawke, their Prime Minister, knew full well Australia had far too big a coastline for her to defend, so sensibly she welcomed the US navy's co operation and the special trade status she has enjoyed ever since.

When you think of those American servicemen who lost their lives in Guada Canal, Tarawa, Okinawa, Iwo Jima and elsewhere, it was no wonder the leader of the opposition in our country exclaimed," I am ashamed to be a New Zealand!" when our Prime Minister gave the US the cold shoulder.

It is no wonder the U.S.A. is taking the war on terror more seriously than any another nation. The whole world has never before been in such a chaotic state. Riots, unrest, protests, civilian deaths in their own streets are rife in many countries. The whole of the Middle East is a powder keg, as in the small nations the young people, many out of work protest in the streets, demanding changes in the leadership of their countries. The British riots, the Norwegian massacre, even the Wall Street protesters are in the headlines. Why is it all happening? The truth is the young people of today are disillusioned with politics, they cannot be blamed if they think the whole world is run on political baloney, they have no jobs they see no future. If they do vote they are never quite sure just what they are voting for. There does not seem to be much sincerity in politics anymore, many an honest dedicated politician enters the fray with such good intentions, hoping to change things for the better, but get caught up in the spiders web of lobbying, corruption, bribery excessive expense accounts, 'pigs in the trough' is the term we use in my country, but it is worldwide. It is so easy to go wrong handling other people's money, whether they be rates, taxes or levies, the money comes rolling in and overzealous, often phoney executives and bureaucrats, a parasitical class if ever there was one, invent grandiose schemes, where they have to raise more money from the already overtaxed, over levied and over rated contributors to justify their predatory existence. Believe me I know because I have been there and seen how they work. Although we had some fantastic executive officers in our organisation, never the less there were bad apples. One of them even embezzled the funds. The President at the time used to sign a whole cheque book leaving it wide open for office staff with sinister intentions.

One such officer could not resist the opportunity, he wrote out a cheque for himself just before the books were closed for the annual audit and then waited to see if the auditors would pick it up. To his great surprise, the auditors missed the transaction and so he spent a whole year fiddling the books then took off overseas before the next audit. I moved that we sack the auditors, but the lawyers, like bankers always ready to protect their own, claiming, 'Oh, you can't do that!".

They even had a much more sophisticated name for it. Instead of embezzlement, they called it. "Defalcation."

That sounds a lot better!! When the fraudster returned to the country he was small fry as to what has taken place in the USA, Europe and Japan when it comes to big time fraud, greed, corruption and bribery. So whoever you are, you had better take the protestors seriously, they have professional members of a rebellious nature among their numbers but the majority are genuine, main-stream, tax payers who have had enough of the politic, skulduggery that prevails in almost every country.

With the population of the planet now seven billion and according to the experts, our breeding proliferation is going to increase another billion every thirteen years, the future is anything but rosy. The main problem is the population increase is happening in poverty-stricken, drought-prone countries that cannot even sustain their present numbers, let alone increase them. However, this is how nature works, if any form of life, human, animals birds, insects and plants show signs of extinction, nature gets goes in an effort to save the species.

As an example, quite some years ago, females in India, as young as eight years old, were reaching puberty and able to bear children. At that time, starvation was rampant in that country and was the main cause of children maturing at an early age – to save the species. Another example is, if a fruit tree has a diseased branch and is going to die, the fruit will ripen on that branch first, long before the rest of the tree so that the stones will be mature enough to germinate to carry on the species. Another classic example is a green pea crop I once grew, the season was so dry, a prolonged drought set in and as I had no water on the property to irrigate, I had to watch agonisingly as my pea crop struggle to only six inches high, burst into flower, but only reduce the tiniest peas I had even seen, containing only two peas in each pod which were of course unsalable. But nature had performed her task of reproduction by just two peas to carry on the survival of the species. This is why it is so hard to stop the excess breeding in many parts of the world that are facing continuous starvation; its nature's response even though a most futile one.

With dwindling supplies of water, food and oil to sustain an out of control population increase; my fear is that the nations will someday fight again to control these vital commodities. If this happens this civilisation will cease to exist as the other nations will be embarking on instant annihilation and it may even be possible for a few well deserved native tribes deep in the jungles of the Amazon or Africa to survive and the person who predicted that cockroaches and a few insects will be the only survivors may be right. It will not be the end of the world, only the world's worst predator.

I had confirmation of this a many years ago when I visited the London Zoo in Regents Park. Within the zoo's compound there is a circular building called the Reptile House, where many of the world's snakes are housed. The magnificent camouflage markings of these reptiles, make it so difficult to ascertain their presence in each of their especially naturally designed undergrowth, in each cubicle.

There was one particular enclosure I was bothered if I could detect any reptile in. However, I did become puzzled at many groups of children who passed by the cubicle and sniggered with laughter at my efforts to detect the occupant. Suddenly I was aware of the reason for their mirth when I read the sign above a full sized mirror that encompassed the entire back wall. It read, 'You are now looking at the World's Worst predator!' I had to laugh at being taken in but could not agree more with the caption, but I did think it a bit rich placing it in the reptile house.

My reason for this assumption was because in reality there are far more nice decent people than there are bad people. There are extremely more people that would help you rather that harm you. The unfortunate souls of this world, who have been dealt a bad hand, are really not to be blamed, as many a wise person has often quoted of an unfortunate who has erred, "There but for the grace of God go I." It is for this very reason why life is a continuous, mysterious unexplainable puzzle. The only factor we are really sure of is that we are here and are struggling to survive. However, we desperately need to rethink the formula because the present one is just not working – it is leading us into oblivion.

The world has always been subject to all kinds of soothsayers, predicting the end of the world, one even claiming it will happen in 2012. But as before, the dated of the predictions come and go and life goes on whole the 'end is nigh,' believers scratch their heads for a future date. The fact is that the world is such a prolific planet and even though the world's worst predator, mankind, has plundered her richest resources, there lies beneath our very feet, under the lithosphere, a colossal bank of replacements that started it all in the first place. There cannot be an end of the world as the many soothsayers predict, but there certainly can be an end to this corrupt civilisation. How and when is unpredictable, whether it maybe super volcanism eruptions blotting out the world, one cannot explain the frailties of behaviour.

As mentioned before, with seven billion people now inhabiting the planet and another billion being added every 13 years, how to sustain this immense increase is going to test the earth to its limits. With millions of young people completing their education annually this is going to put pressure on an already overstretched workforce that is struggling to cope. The revolt in small countries in the Middle East who have either assassinated or changed their leaders are still no better off, as new, well intentioned, would be saviours, try to restore order to an almost ungovernable population who have been treated so harshly in the past. Even Europe and the U.S.A. have their share of protestors, tax payer's revolt, irresponsible banks under constant investigation, yet opposing any kind of banking regulations that would hamper their fraudulent systems. The whole western world had never ever before been in such financial chaos and no one seems to know how to solve this fiscal dilemma. While genuine attempts are being made to solve this problem and avoid a worldwide slump.

There are some people who are already preparing for such a disaster. I saw recently on T.V, some well-off Americans in a remote area in the USA, setting up substantial stocks of canned and dried food, shelved like a miniature supermarket. On top of all this uncertainty, the international situation is not that stable as we have two time bombs ticking away.

One is in the Middle East where an Iranian despotic leader is determined to wipe Israel off the map. He continually claims he is not making a nuclear device. Hitler also claimed he only wanted peace – but what he really meant was a little piece of Poland and a big piece of Europe! If this little up-start, already drunk with power by the concern he has created, achieves his aim, he will have the means to activate Armageddon in the Middle East. I cannot for the life of me, understand why he has not been taken out by the United Nations or N.A.T.O. I only hope they know what they are doing and are not procrastinating like the Western Alliance did in the 1930's, when they let Hitler break the Treaty of Versailles time and time again, for six years. They finally declared war on him when they were so unprepared and really not in a position to do so. In 1939 Britain trained her recruits in Hyde Park with broom handles and walking sticks! – the same as they did in 1914. There is a saying that predicts that those who do not look back and learn from the past mistakes are destined to repeat them.

Then there is the second time bomb – North Korea who is longing for a nod from Big Daddy to fire his missiles. This equally explosive area, the South China Sea, has huge oil reserves claimed by several nations bordering the area. Why fight for it and have a blood bath around the Stratly Islands, where all the oil will be lost and nobody will win. The solution to this area where everyone is claiming ownership is to form a consortium oil company of all the claimants and allocate the oil according to the population of the countries involved. Mind you it would have to be chaired or run by someone as astute as Lee Kuan Yew, to avoid any corruption or political skulduggery. It is just a thought, but think of all the lives and devastation it would save, as well as all the oil which the area so sorely needs.

I can well imagine any member of one of the smaller nations claiming jurisdiction over the oil reserves and who may be unfortunate to read this epistle, screaming from the top of the tallest oilrig, "Unworkable! Impossible! Ridiculous and anyway, why should China, the richest country in the world, get the lion's share?"

My answer would be because she has the largest population and therefore the greatest need. Anyway, the field is open for anyone else to come up with a better scheme; and the United Nations will buy it, I'm sure anything to avoid another blood bath in the Pacific. Past history informs us all that nations have fought for much lesser reasons than black gold.

We must all remember the famous words of President J.F. Kennedy, when he said,

"If man cannot end war, then war will end mankind!"

SAVING CAPITALISM

Chapter 12

Throughout the whole 95 years I have been round, I have never been able to find out just how the world's financial system really works. Banker and Accountants who I have approached and who you would think would know, could not explain it, only to inform me that it was corrupt.

Politicians certainly have no idea otherwise they would not place their countries into such huge deficits. President Clinton could not fathom the finance riddle and he would not have exploded when he was informed by his financial advisors that his Re-election depended on the action of the country's Bond Traders. Despite all the hiccups in his tenure, you have to give him full credit – he balanced the budget. If ever the secretive fraudulent financial system of the world was revealed on just how it works to the ordinary type of Joe Blogs like me, the whole world would be in an uproar. Perhaps this is part of the reason we are witnessing a taxpayer revolt in many western countries today, occupying Wall St and elsewhere. The general public are looking for the answers - all they are seeking is the truth – a rare commodity in these turbulent times. When a single bank can print 3 trillion in bank notes without any asset backing, it makes you wonder. How does it all work? Bond Traders, Currency Dealers, Merchant Bankers, Stockbrokers, Inside Traders, Finance Houses, Loan Sharks, and Banks must be taking the Western World to the cleaners, according to all the frauds and collapse of finance companies that have been revealed since the fiscal melt down. Any wonder we have programmes on TV like 'Squawk Box Europe' and

Max Keisers "No Holds Barred" comments that enlighten us all of the financial skulduggery that is taking place daily under our very noses. You should not be able to deal in another country's currency, why can't the exchange rate be the same in every country, so that hard working exporters and manufacturers are not penalised? I can well imagine the eyebrows I will have raised in financial circles at such pertinent queries.

We had a couple of bank tellers in our country, cotton onto the merchant bank bonanza. They left their bank and went into the Merchant Banking Business and made so much money, so quickly, they had to seek a tax haven. But a smart politician blew the whistle and they had to skip the country. However, they were small fry compared to the huge fraudulent dealings and financial collapses overseas. When most of our little country's finance companies went belly up recently, and thousands of pensioners lost their life savings, some of their executives went to jail, but others still had million dollar birthday bashes and kept on building a $35 million home; while some of their pensioner victims had to go back to work to survive. Banks and Finance Companies, simply oppose any regulations - it limits their operations, curbs their greed and stifles their appetite for the endless profit! Banks were not so hungry in the olden days. The days of the family Bank Manager are long gone. Just like the Family Lawyer and the Family Accountant and the Family Doctor; although I still enjoy the last two mentioned. There is a new breed out there and they are really hungry. In the olden days, we revered our bank Managers – we looked up to them. But now some branches have no managers and I thank God I'm in a position to tell them to jump in the lake if I don't get the service I am entitled to as a customer. When currency dealers speculate against the Dollar, the Euro or the Pound; and make millions, they had produced nothing. On the other hand, a Baker works all night and by morning he has produced thousands of loaves of bread for his customers. Farmers produce food for a hungry world. A manufacturer turns out countless goods that are in constant demand. A carpenter borrows from his bank and then works long hours building a lovely home. The result of all this hard work and investment is something tangible that is a great contribution to the economy of any country; whole on the other hand, predatorial speculators in currency transactions are an impediment to the economy. They may have made millions, but some banks or Governments must have lost millions they cannot afford to lose. The hours spent each day in currency and financial speculation is the world's largest casino and is the ultimate in the abuse of capitalism.

The reason I have made all these observations and comments is solely because I am worried about the future of capitalism. Millions of other capitalist in the western countries, far more intelligent than I, are equally concerned and are searching for answers. Ever since the financial collapse of irresponsible banks and fraudulent finance companies; capitalism has been under scrutiny. Suggestions that the Western Nations have had their day cannot be brushed aside if capitalism cleans up its act and eliminates the predators. If it does not do anything about it, these financial parasites will cause the demise of capitalism, which will self destruct and all these ultra wealthy speculators will take off to their tax havens, leaving the rest of the community to cope with the economic chaos they will have caused and left behind. Unless all hard working capitalists can band together and put an end to this corrupt antiquated system, Max Keizer's prediction of the 'Four Horsemen', may come true.

It is impossible to predict or even contemplate the outcome of the present ongoing financial saga; as there appears to be not the slightest glimpse of light at the end of the fiscal tunnel. Tough measures currently being imposed by the banks in Cyprus are only the tip of the financial iceberg as to what lies ahead. The recent revelations from the USA that some of their bans maybe too big to prosecute, causing a panellist to comment that the lunatics were now in charge of the Asylum. Such a statement was the gist for the mill to Max Kreisler of the "no holds barred" of the Kreisler report. However, it all goes to prove that capitalism has to be reinvented if it is to be saved from self destruction, despite their cries of pain and protestation from banks and the financial sector are going to have to become strictly regulated and all those who oppose such measures will place themselves in the category of the fraudsters who were responsible for this gigantic fiscal crisis in the first place. If the

Western nations keep bungling on as they are continually doing, there is nothing to save capitalism, then China will do it for them and then the cat will be really among the pigeons. As a humble tiller of the soil, and not that long off the turnips so to speak, although I have almost 96 years on the clock and am still working and loving it, not making much money as I no longer have to, I mainly work to stay fit and healthy; as Prime Minister Gladstone, in England, said years ago when urging his constituents to work harder, "Hard work never killed anyone! It will not kill me because I don't do any!" Joking aside, it is my view that the west handed the world on a plate to the Chinese and the majority of those hard working people grasped it with both hands and turned their country into the economic miracle it is today. It is going to be interesting to see how they handle prosperity or if they fall victim to that malignant western disease called, "Extravagance", which has so recently placed so many western nations on the brink of bankruptcy, all the result of 60 continuous years of prosperity, overspend, over borrowing, living far beyond their income; the evidence cause and effect are so obvious a blind man could detect it. Only time will tell, as history, which has a habit of repeating itself, will prove. I only hope capitalism, the honest variety, can be saved. Some of my friends think not, but I still have hope and a policy of never giving up. The reason I suppose is I have 16 grandchildren and 23 great grandchildren and still counting; it is their future and all the rest of the world's young people I am concerned about. All capitalism needs is tough, honest, sincere politicians who cannot be bought, then saving capitalism would be far more achievable. As I write this chapter, fate has just destined me to view a program on TV called, "Squawk Box Europe", which invites panellists from all sectors, right and left and centre and all of the horror of the banks, burglars and Governments. As the guest speaker enlightened ordinary folk, like me, just what is going on in this crazy world of high finance? The program, I have just seen, consisted of a much switched on lady who made a great effort to define capitalism; also an aged gentleman who had a different view of capitalism. The third panellist was an extremely biased socialist. It was very enlightening, but I was horrified at the end when the host, who had given the socialist the final comment, made the astonishing statement, claiming that at the time of the financial meltdown in 2008, the Government lent the banks enormous amounts of money for the bailouts, free of interest and the banks, then lent the money back to the Government at interest; and according to the panellist, pocketed the profit! I was further amazed that neither of the other panellists commented on that statement. It seemed to me like a financial version of Alice in Wonderland! If this actually happened (and I find it hard to believe) Government's should be prevented from handling tax −payer's money, as they are just not responsible. With such a revelation it looks as if the road back is going to be long and hard, with economic pain for everyone, but it will be worth it. Capitalism just has to be revived, but with regulations. We all hate regulations but we have strict regulations when we drive on our roads or we would all be killed; why not then can tough regulations be imposed on finance to save us all from being killed economically!

Ever since the financial meltdown in 2008, the issue of cause and effect have been hotly debated throughout most of the western economies. Yet, not a single person Government or anyone from the secretive, corrupt world of high finance have come up with a solution to rescue the near bankrupt western countries from this fiscal quagmire. It is perhaps understandable that a solution could not be expected from the high finance sector as it would not end their longstanding, lucrative, bonanza from whence they could transfer their immense profits to their already over bulging overseas tax-haven accounts. It would be most interesting to know just how many tax havens there are in the world. I have just heard the island of Tonga, in the Pacific, has become a tax haven. If such tax dodging financial hideaways keep escalating, western governments will suffer and even greater reduction in revenue that they are receiving today. Dysfunctional tax systems of many European countries, which contributes to their near bankrupt state is threatening the survival of the European Union. Perhaps the Union is overstretched and is too big with so many members not pulling their weight and letting the side down. It will be a continuous struggle for it to survive. If countries like Spain can get away with stashing 21 trillion away in overseas tax havens, then expect to be bailed out by the other member countries, then who pays their taxes?

The many years of futile attempts of tax collectors from around the world to ascertain the names of depositors and their deposits in the many tax havens is evidence enough to prove just how sinister these financial deposits really are. The fact that they want to keep it all clouded in secrecy, suggests guilt! Bill Gates does not mind disclosing his wealth. He is not afraid of paying tax. His entrepreneurial success is capitalism at its best, the honest kind! His tax haven is the American economy to which he has made such a great contribution.

I am only a soil man and know little about the fraudulent methods of high finance, only to know it is corrupt and the cause of the western countries fiscal dilemma. With no solution coming from such important organisations as the World Bank or the International Monetary Fund, whom would you think could solve this vexing problem. Seeing that the whole world has opted for globalisation, would not a Global Currency prevent such a reoccurrence of what we are all going through? It is only a suggestion. The currency dealers and bond traders would have nightmares of course, but better for them to be upset than the hardworking producer exporter, who constantly sees their returns shrinking as the overseas exchange rate fluctuates wildly, making their exporting operations unviable. The bailouts for the countries like Greece and Cyprus are only temporary sedatives, not a solution and will have to be repeated again and again; and which will encourage other cash strapped countries to line up for handouts as they head for the fiscal cliff we constantly hearing about. The strange state of this present recession (and I have experienced many) is that everything is still so expensive which makes it especially hard for folk on fixed incomes or unemployed. We have a large number of people out of work in my country, yet, the Government has just allowed 7000 Philippi no's into the country to work in the Dairy industry. Kiwis do not like to work 7 days a week. Dairy cows do not know about 40 hour weeks, so if you do not milk them on Saturday and Sunday they will cease to give milk on a Monday or Tuesday and go dry. So now we are going to have Phillapino's milking our cows and Indians picking our apple crops, while Kiwis are in the dole! I remember the first depression in 1922; I was just a boy then so it did not affect me as long as I received my one penny per week, to buy acid drops or black balls which would last the whole week if I was careful. Everyone seemed poor in those days, only the storekeeper, the butcher and he Doctor had a big house, but only the Doctor had a car. My father used to hire a horse and gig to take the family for an outing on a Sunday. He used to call the horse, "Desert Gold after a champion racehorse owned by Mrs Perry, a Maori Princess who sold Ohurakura Indigenous Native Bush to Robert Holt and Sons for 70,000 pounds – equivalent to well over $200,000,000 today. Then came the Big Depression of the thirties that followed the 1929 Wall Street Crash, which lasted six years in our country, but longer in other countries. Inflation became rampant after the Second World War, as too much money was chasing too fewer goods. The numerous recessions that have occurred since the end of the Second World War especially after the oil shock, have been short in duration but this present downturn, with so many western countries near bankruptcy, and unable to stem the escalation of their debt, the duration and final outcome is unpredictable. With no end and no sign of a solution, at least there should be a concerted effort but all the nations involved to design an economic formula to prevent any reoccurrence of a similar fiscal disaster we are at present suffering. It may be a big ask, but all the public require is honesty! Honesty in Government, honesty in business. but most of all, honesty in the world of finance! It must be remembered that today's public are being enlightened daily by the constant TV news and political, business and financial information it keeps them so well informed as to what is taking place and while they might not understand fully just what is on, they know that there are a lot of cover ups of political international and financial shady manoeuvres, hence taxpayers revolt and mayhem in the streets which not only make things worse, but do nothing to solve the problem. Never the less, the day of enlightenment is with us, so the authorities are going to have to come clean; completely cleanse the financial system or the Four Horsemen will soon be keeping their appointment with destiny and the sinister world of finance will become a clean slate!

Is there any possible way the four horsemen's rendezvous with destiny could be impeded and thus prevent the demise of the western nations by their fiscal dilemma? Ever since the 2008 financial meltdown, when greed, fraud in high places and irresponsible banking was exposed and capitalism had to be bailed out by Socialism, there have been countless deals with debates on cause and effect; but no solution, despite the best brains from all the western nations taking part. Many talk about kick starting the economy as if it was a motor bike, but the west's economic motor bike has run out of gas! Socialists are calling for more growth, they cannot seem to get it onto their heads that the growth has gone to India and China – so have the jobs! Whenever there is a gigantic economic crisis, as we are confronted with today, there are always many contributing factors - not the least being in this present crisis, human behaviour, which as I keep quoting, "defies analysis". Globalisation has also played an immense part in shifting jobs from the West to the East and you are not going to get them back! A well known popular make of British tractor (I have had nine of them) are now made in India. Such a move must affect jobs in the United Kingdom. Furthermore, most of the Western nations are suffering from an overdose of continuous prosperity and again as I have already quoted," prosperity is much harder to cope with than adversity." Complacency sets in, high living, easy money, excess welfare, irresponsibility; all combine to contribute to a decadent society, that riot, burn and protest at the slightest form of austerity that is imposed to correct the downturn. Such spoilt, ruined people do not know how to cope with adversity – it is just not in their vocabulary. The European Union's is a typical example - some members have broken the rules by taking advantage of the Unions success and have borrowed and lived beyond their country's income and now have to be bailed out at the prudent members expense. Once you bail out a dilatory country, you will have to keep on with futile bailouts as they probably have a dysfunctional tax system, so will never be able to pay their own way. The European Union's may have just got too big and cumbersome. Countries that have got themselves into massive, uncontrollable debt, have only one solution – they have to place their Administration on a war footing – form a coalition Government by giving up the luxury of costly, unnecessary elections, all work together as a team to get their country back on track. It worked in the Second World War, it will work again now. Of course a few, if any will buy it simply because they cannot comprehend the seriousness of the situation that could end in revolution and anarchy, as the west continues to stampede towards the financial precipice we are supposed to be heading to. The first step is to stop printing money, which is not even a sedative! It is like chemotherapy is to cancer – it slows down the disease, but kills the patient. The next step is to stop living beyond your income. I know the medicine and pain will be horrific for the bureaucrats, but there is no alternative. Even hardworking Germany, the leading economy in Europe with an efficient tax system and the country that turns out the finest quality goods in the world, is between a rock and a hard place. All the ailing, no- hoper countries like Greece, Spain, Portugal, Ireland, Italy and soon to join them, France; who have let the side down, have the impression Germany can bail them out. How can one country carry so many spend-thrift economies? Yet if she doesn't, the European Union is finished! No wonder the United Kingdom retained the pound! They might just be able to resuscitate it, and it will be Prime Minister Cameron's fault if they don't. With 40 million on food stamps in the richest economy in the world and their deficit now seventeen trillion and climbing in the USA., surely, this once great country is not going to spend another four years of political bickering, blaming each other instead of working together to halt the slide into a deeper financial abyss. The whole world has never been as unstable as it is today. Even India and China will not be immune from a western economic collapse, as they both depend on western markets. Of course, they will weather the economic depression far better than the wet as they know how to cope with adversity; whereas the western nations do not, especially their young people who have only known good times and so much prosperity, luxurious living, full employment, never having to want for anything -instant gratification. Adversity is not in their vocabulary, so when their Government tries to impose a little austerity they scream in pain, protest, riot, burn and loot, which only makes things worse. It all goes to prove how prosperity can be the mother of failure and failure can be the cause of success. Take how many Empires have fallen over the centuries, through over indulgence in luxurious living and extravagance -The Assyrians, the Greeks, the Hapsburgs, the Ottomans and quite recently the British Empire. The Roman Empire lasted 400 years, but the British Empire hardly made 250 years. – Two World Wars finished her off. Perhaps the days of empires, kingdoms and dynasties are over and all to the good of mankind. The strange thing about humanity is that wherever there are people, there are problems and the more people, the greater are the problems. Now with 7 billion of us and another billion every 13 years, it is hard to imagine what lies ahead. Take the Middle East countries, like Egypt and Libya have ousted their dictatorial leaders for new democratic ones. But their problems are not solved simply because they have no industry and so no jobs – evidently oil is not enough in Libya to correct the situation. The entire world has never ever had so much unemployment and it is going to get worse as robots and modern technology increase. When people are not wanted they don't feel so good and thus you perceive deterioration in character. But when a person has a job, they have to perform and they strive to honour that position. It gives satisfaction of a job well done, being your own boss, however is an even greater challenge. There is a greater risk investment to be made and still greater competition, but if successful, greater satisfaction and rewards. I suppose there will always be the great friction between labour and management. I could be quite wrong but in this view, but I came to the conclusion early on in life, that tough workers were the cause of tough bosses and tough bosses were the cause of tough workers, which really means that both are to blame. Unions can be so powerful, they can wreck an industry and as for union bosses, they can be impossible to negotiate with! When a union receive a substantial pay rise, through strike or negotiation, who do you think pays for it in the long run? Not the company who already has huge overheads. They have to raise their prices to pay for the pay rise; therefore it is the poor consumer who gets penalised. All those unfortunate workers on fixed incomes and pensioners, who can ill afford to pay such extra costs. It is all a vicious on-going circle that commerce and Government and the public have to cope with; and which also contributes to inflation. We had two of the largest freezing works in the country; close their doors for ever, in part, due to the difficulty in negotiation with the unions. They were too big. The bigger the industry, the more powerful the unions become and so the more trouble. Look at the Teamsters Union in the USA, they were so big and powerful, they were huge money lenders. Remember Jimmy Hoffa, sent to jail for some union problem – when he was released and demanded his old job back as head of the Teamsters Union, he kept an appointment with some members and was never seen again! Water-siders caused more delays to shipping and industry in my country than any other union. One year when my young family had been working hard all though the tomato season, picking and packing tomatoes, at the end of the last week of the school holidays, I decided to take the family to Auckland for the opening of the International Airport. We stayed at a lovely motel overlooking the harbour. On the Friday before the opening, I took them for a drive across the harbour bridge to the North Shore. On returning, as we approached the lights at the bottom of Queens' street, the lights changed to red, so we had to stop. The pedestrian buzzer went and a large group of water-siders, who had been lunching at the bar of the nearby hotel, began to cross in front of our latest Pontiac car painted beautiful, slaty, chicory blue. It really did look magnificent – all bought and earned by the hard work of my wife, seven children and me. A huge water-sider with a monstrous tummy came over to the car and thumped the bonnet so hard, I thought he had dented it and said, "If you had to work for a living like we do, you would not own a car like this!" My wife was furious! That water-sider was looking at one of the hardest working teams in the country and that is why we owned such a car. It was team work – something the water-sider would never understand. Such is the mentality of some workers. But thank God, they are not all like that. One of the largest mills was on strike caused by a tough English Union boss. The head of the firm locked the gates and said to the workers looking on, "Let's know when you want to come back to work." The strike went on and on – no money for food, for the children, the wives began blaming the union boss, who hightailed it off back to England, never to be seen again. I remember when Lee Iacocca borrowed millions off the USA Government to revive the Chrysler Car Company. He did a deal with the unions, who were astute enough to comprehend less reckoning and look what happened to the automotive workers, jobs were saved, so was the Chrysler Company and Lee paid the Government back the loan before it was due. They were so pleased with Lee they asked him to stand for president, but Lee declined.-he was much too astute to accept. He knew how to fix Chrysler but a whole country was asking too much. There was a time in the USA that auto workers were receiving 22 dollars per hour when Japanese auto workers were receiving 12 dollars per hour. No wonder Japan captured the world's car market. There must be easily 80% of the cars and trucks in my country made in Japan and that is why I can no longer buy a Pontiac or Ford. So the question has to be asked, 'Has the demand of tough union bosses played at least in some part in the switch to robotics and so put the masses out of work?"

There will be no turning the clock back, like in China and India; those jobs have gone for good! A leaf should be taken out of the German book of Industrial relations. Their industry consult with the unions all the cards are laid on the table and judging by German's success, it must be working. The burning question is of course," How long can the west go on borrowing to avoid an economic depression that will make the slump of the '30s look like a Sunday School Picnic?" What would happen if China called in her loans? Perhaps she realises it might be like shooting themselves in the foot – I really just do not know. One can only admire China as an economic success. They have proved that no one can bar the path of a country whose people utilise most of their waking hours for work. Of course, China's greatest challenge will come when a greater proportion of her population become skilled workers which will necessitate even greater access to the world's markets. China's ability to cope with adversity has been proved over the centuries. She is about to prove she can handle prosperity and all its destructive challenges that tempt the greedy, the corrupt and the fraudsters that finally undermine a stable economy. Already China is taking a long hard look at the first sign of a western disease with the symptoms such as extravagance. China can learn a lot from the west as to how to handle it. The cancerous financial disease that has hit many western nations, who are at their wits end as to how to cope with it, has almost reached the malignant stage where they are treating it with financial chemotherapy, such as continuous bail-outs and printing money, which is disastrous. The only cure is that unpopular, difficult to swallow medicine, called, "Austerity". Some countries have been forced to impose this undesirable treatment only to have their recipients scream in pain at such harsh measures and react by street protests, rioting and burning property – all which makes their ailing economy much worse. It is easy for the authorities and well off people to condemn these unfortunate people who are out of work, but when they see grinning bank executives who have just been fired for malpractice in a banks operation and leave with a huge bonus, for perhaps losing as much as a billion dollars, one can only sympathises with their concerns; and the west can expect more of the same, unless they can clean up their antiquated financial systems, regulate the banks, so that it all works for everyone and not for a greedy few, who are responsible for this fiscal disaster. All the main street people and small capitalists like me, want is the truth, all the financial cards on the table; sincerity in politics, don't laugh – I'm serious! Do away with big Government - we have a shocking form of democracy – it is really bureaucracy and is why a lot of people all over the western world, do not vote. They know whoever wins; they are only going to get more of the same. Millions in the USA and millions of pro Americans, like me, outside American are really concerned. The world needs a strong America in both security and economy. If there are people wondering why the USA has so many supporters outside America, it is simply because many folk of my generation have not forgotten and are still immensely grateful for the USA's massive contribution and sacrifice made by their country in freeing Europe and turning back the Japanese invasion of the Pacific in the 1940's; with such a huge loss of life. With two loose cannons – one in Iran and the other in North Korea, where both leaders seemed determined to bring about the destruction of their countries, the economic disaster confronting the west would fade into insignificance if these two hotheads were to set the world alight.

GLOBAL WARMING

Chapter 13

The debate that has taken place in the past few years on this controversial subject, without any definite conclusion, has prompted its advocates to accept defeat and alter the name change to "Climate Change". With such a hung jury on the case, this name is far more acceptable as we all know that the climate around the world has been changing for millions of years and will never ever cease to change despite mankind's puny contribution by way of pollution. Volcanic eruptions belch millions of tonnes of sulphur dioxide onto the atmosphere each year that make mankind s contributions insignificant. Ever since global warming was first mooted, I have never met one person who believes in the theory, though many sought my opinion. I kept an open mind for some time until I saw Al Gore on television one evening make in his final summary the claim that it was for this reason that the Pacific Islanders were all immigrating to New Zealand as the seas were flooding their habitat. The Pacific Islanders come to New Zealand for the fright lights, the jobs and the benevolent welfare state, we offer. Furthermore, their islands, many of which are extremely low lying, have been eroding by immense Pacific storms, as are many coastal areas in continents around the world and definitely not to rising sea water. Some islands in the Pacific are protected by coral reefs that act as a buffer and prevent erosion. Others are not so fortunate. Sadly, it is a fact of life, that whenever a trendy cause is suggested to an eager but ignorant public, like the nuclear free or global warming or in my country, anti-smacking of children, legislation by the Green Party and lowering the drinking age by a right wing, lady Prime Minister (hard to believe such a woman would be so naive), Politicians, desperate to hold on to their slender majority, latch onto these unproven, risky changes. Consequently, in our country with the anti-smacking legislation, we have children throwing chairs at teacher, parents being taken to court by their children, as discipline has been abolished. The lower drinking age legislation of course is far more serious as binge drinking by teenagers escalates causing the police an impossible task to control. A recent party, that went online, attracted 500 youngsters and that resulted in injuries arrests and damage to police vehicles. So far politicians have failed to reinstate the higher drinking age for fear of losing votes. It would be for the good of the country and the well being of the people they should legislate for, not for votes.

As with the anti-smacking bill, it was brought in to prevent child abuse and helpless little babies being killed. It has not had the slightest effect. Stepfathers or in most cases, step – partners are still taking the lives of these helpless little ones.

I sincerely hope that other countries may learn from our ridiculous legislation.

So, with some of the coldest winters ever experienced in Europe and North America, trendy global warming has been finally put to rest, and to the relief of all our country's dairy cows, which were going to be taxed on all their excreta, can breathe a sigh of relief, that that ridiculous legislation will not be revived.

It is never ending the way the legislators leave no stone unturned to think up ways and means to impose severe taxes on producers to contain the spendthrift policies.

JACK DUNN

Chapter 14

All through the 80years of producing and marketing horticultural produce, I had the good fortune to employ a great many wonderful helpers, many of whom became friends for life. Husband and wife teams and one such union we ended up share cropping as they had access to saline land that with such a history of marine life, contained all the vital minerals and trace elements that produce the finest tomatoes and winter keeping pumpkins possible. I had markets screaming for the produce so our combination paid great dividends. However, there was one employee I must pay special tribute to, for his wonderful philosophical outlook and a spirit that defies description. He was a retired farmer in his seventies who was still fit and healthy, but bored with nothing to do. He had a couple of race horses, I do not know if he ever raced them, but that was his only interest. I always wished I could have taken him to see the Melbourne Cup, but November was one of our busiest months of the year. His name was John Stirling, known as Jack Dunn and a finer gentleman as ever you could wish to meet.

Jack Dunn was born to Scottish parents who emigrated from Scotland around 1860, and settled in Christchurch, in the South Island of New Zealand. The Scots seemed to favour the lower part of the South Island for settling, I suppose it reminded them of Bonnie Scotland, as the area is bounded by huge lakes and snow-capped mountains. Well before the turn of the century, Jack's father bought a large sheep and cattle farm in the back country of Hawkes Bay, a province on the east coast of the North Island. When Jack's father told a friend, a Mr Ballin, of his purchase, his friend, replied, "Well, it will be the making of your boys, but it will do nothing for your girls!"

When Jack revealed this episode to me over 70 years later, I queried,

"Was Mr Ballin's prediction correct?"

And Jack confirmed that it was. When the family arrived on the farm, which was in the remote district of Puketitiri, a timber mill settlement, Jack was just 12 years old and had just left school. He was keen to start working on the farm as there was so much to do like ploughing the land to grow crops, of oats for feed for the large Clydesdale draught horses that the farmer required to clear the land; also the cows to be fed, sheep to be shorn, lambs to be docked, so more hands the better. Imagine Jack's disgust when they found that the one roomed school was short of one pupil to qualify for a teacher and Jack had to go back to school to make up the numbers. As the boys in the family grew to maturity, the farm could not sustain the number of son's, so Jack took a job on a big sheep and cattle station over the province's mountain range, called Ohoako. But the day Jack arrived to work; all the station hands were on strike. They were demanding butter on their bread! Up until then, they had had only treacle, which was known as bullocky's joy. They asked Jack if he was going to join them in the strike. Jack informed them that he had accepted the billet as it was, so he couldn't very well strike the day he arrived so therefore, unable to join the strike which seemed fair enough. Later, Jack was to take on a large bush block in the King Country in the middle of the North Island, then finally to return home and take over the family farm at Puketitiri. At the end of the Second World War, he was now in his 70's and the farm was getting too much for him and his wife as they had no children. They decided to sell out. After managing a small block, where he fattened cattle for a large station, Jack retired but became bored with nothing to do, so he came to work for me. At that time, we were buying up small properties for cropping where there were a lot of old fences to be dismantled which suited Jack fine.

Jack never owned a car, was too old to learn to ride a bicycle – the old chap kept falling off. He had only conquered horses, draughts and hacks. He was an expert horseman. So when my wife took the children to school, she picked him up off the bus. Jack thought the world of our children. He was like a grandfather to them all. When our daughter, Carolyn won a Country Girls' competition on cropping and horticulture, he came to work the next day with an open cheque and said, "Here, take this. Christine (our youngest daughter) should go over with you."

We had an enormous task to try and convince him that it was not possible for Christine to go, as Carolyn would be staying with sugar cane grower's families and vegetable growers, who may not be able to accommodate two extra people. Jack was most upset and disappointed that Christine could not accompany her sister. Bringing an open cheque for Christine was typical of Jack's generosity and his outlook on life itself. On one occasion, when the markets were over supplied and the family were all enjoying our beach home, I asked Jack to take a couple of weeks off and gave him 2 weeks holiday pay. At the end of that day, before he knocked off, he came to me with the cheque and said,

"Here, take this. I have never, ever been paid for doing nothing and am not going to start now." Despite my protests that it was the law, he would not accept the cheque.

My barber said to me one day, when he was cutting my hair, "You know that elderly gentleman that works for you, when I am cutting his hair, he tells me all about the wonderful crops you grow and all the nice things about your family. He talks like a young man and I think it must be because he is working with such young and positive people. He is a joy to talk to. On the other hand, I have had customers in here, ten to fifteen years younger, who complain about their aches and pains, so much they leave me totally depressed! But not Jack, he always says how busy 'we' all are and the great production that results."

When we were harvesting potatoes, Jack sewed up all the bags as they were filled and placed them back on the ground. It was an ideal light job for him to do and it really made him feel part of the team, as he was an expert with the needle and string. With our first mechanical harvester, the potatoes were bagged at the back of the machine and then placed on the ground, not like our later machines that held them on a platform, hence when it was time to load up, all hands threw the full bags up to the stacker on the truck, and our 7 tonner had a rather high deck. Jack would insist he should help load and wanted to prove at 80, he was just as good as my boys and me. Not to offend him, I used to shake my head to Barry, who was stacking, so he would call out, "Jack would you mind picking up the empties?" There used to be the odd empty bag left on the ground. If, at odd times there were no empties, to stop Jack from the heavy lifting, Barry would throw a few empties back on the ground when Jack wasn't looking, just to stop him from loading.

One day when we were picking up a load with a smaller truck, our three- tonner, to stop Jack from doing any lifting, he was so keen to help, I asked him, if he would try driving the truck. He was a little reluctant at first and suggested, "No, you drive and I'll help load."

"No, No," I replied,"Hop in, it's easy, I'll show you."

So Jack sat behind the wheel and I pointed to the left pedal and said,

"That's the clutch, push it to the floor, put the gear level over to the left, let the clutch out, slowly and you're away. If you want to stop, push the pedal to the floor and pull the gear lever back to neutral."

The rows were well over two hundred metres long, so no harm could be done. In the lowest gear, Jack took off, while we all loaded the potatoes - all Jack had to do was steer. As we approached the far boundary fence, to make it easy for Jack, I hopped on the running board and said,

"Get ready to put your foot on the clutch and press it to the floor."

However, when Jack saw the fence approaching, he panicked and called out, "Whoa, whoa!"

He was back on the farm with his Clydesdales, so I had to lean over and switch the engine off to save the fence, while Barry had to hold his load with both arms at the sudden stop. I had to stop the boys from laughing at Jack calling out for the truck to stop at his command, even though it was humorous. Later, that year, Jack now being well into his eighties, he was keen as ever still to work. It was sometimes difficult to find jobs for him in winter. Some mornings when it was pouring with rain, the phone would ring at 5.00am.

"What's on today?" Jack would query.

"Is it not raining at your place? I would ask Jack.

"Oh, it's only the pride of the morning," Jack would reply. "It will be over by 10.00am".

He so wanted to work. Most wet days in the winter, we spent cleaning and brushing Winter Keeping pumpkins. If the market was right, then Jack was a great help at that task, it was during these days we used to get into great discussions about the world affairs, politics, religion, war, high finance etc. He hated war and reckoned that they were caused by bad politics, power struggles, high finances and trade. He was beginning to doubt the benefits of capitalism and seemed extremely interested in Russia's venture into communism and also China's. He passed away before the USSR 70 year experiment collapsed. He would have been amazed at the political hybridisation of communism and capitalism and the enormous prosperity it has created in that country.

Jack always claimed that during the Napoleonic Wars, the Rothschild's Banks in Paris, London and Berlin, all kept both the French and the British army's well supplied with funds when either ran out. He even brought me a book on the Rothschild's to prove it; and then borrowed it off me to see if he was right. No one really knows what goes on behind the scenes with international finances during a world war. I have just witnessed a documentary on television, where a commentator claimed that an international German Bank, helped fund the British Second World War effort, even though both countries were at war with each other! That is mind bloggling. Surely Hitler would not have known this. If he had found out, he would have surely closed it down and put the whole staff in a concentration camp!

So Jack's disillusionment with politics, capitalism and war might well be understandable. He endured real hard times farming in the back country, two wars and the 1930's depression. He used to tell me how he drove a large mob of sheep 46 miles, over a dry, dusty, hilly road to the sale yards and then drive them back home because they did not sell. No stock trucks in those days. He knew his bible well and often quoted it to me during many of our discussions. He was convinced that the Jew's were God's chosen people. I told him I did not agree at all with that theory. I maintained that God was on the side of everything, even the bugs, viruses and the bacteria. He just used to smile at my views. Working the soil and being close to nature was where my information came from. One day after my wife had taken Jack down to the bus after picking the children up from school; she came to me and said, "You'll really have to retire Mr Dunn. He went to sleep in the car going home. It really must be too much for him."

I informed her how difficult it would be as it would destroy him. I would have to be very careful how I told him. So I chose the end of January, our main summer month, when the markets became oversupplied with excess produce from the growers on the highly productive plains. At that time we had a lovely beach house where we fished and surfed, so I told him we wanted him to spend some time out there while things were slack. He was not too pleased, but accepted the situation reluctantly. Sometime later, when I was passing his home, I dropped in some fruit and vegetables. His wife met me at the door and I queried how Jack was. Just then he appeared around the corner of the house and I got the shock of my life. He had aged 10 years. I could not believe his appearance. Mrs Dunn pleaded with me,

"Can't you find a job, he is driving me silly?"

Jack was well into his eighties by now, so to save his life I took him back on but on reduced days. He picked up his spirit and appearance immediately and was still working for us in his 90th year. One evening, when he was out on the road, picking up his evening papers, a car was passing his place and was overtaken by another which drove onto Jack's side of the road with its lights dipped and did not see Jack as he bent down to retrieve his papers. The car threw him up, over the bonnet and into the windshield, smashing one leg, an arm and his face. His leg was so badly mangled that it had to come off. When I first went to see him, he was still full of spirit and enthusiasm.

"What do you think of losing a leg, just when I'm in my prime of life?"

When my youngest son, Mark went in to visit, he smiled and said,

"Hello, Mark, do you think your dad will still have a job up there for an old, one legged cuss?"

Yes, he still wanted to come back to work with only one leg. Jack had his 90th birthday in hospital and my daughter, Carolyn baked him a big birthday cake which we all took up to him in hospital and gave him a bottle of his favourite whiskey, which of course was given to the nurses for when he was discharged. When Jack finally came out of hospital, he just could not cope with the artificial limb and was confined to a wheelchair. He passed away a couple of years later. We heard later that on his deathbed he had called,

"Where are the Claytons?"

A truly wonderful man with such a great sense of values and a tremendous spirit.

Printed in the United States
By Bookmasters